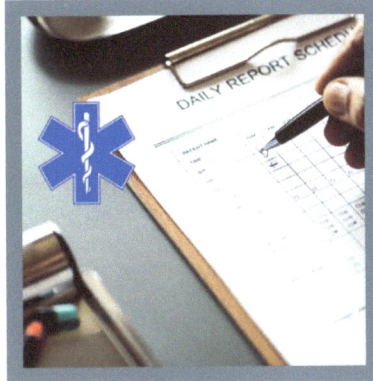

Business Process Management in Healthcare Organizations

About this Book

Some readers prefer a brief overview before reading a book. Others prefer no overview – they want to jump right into the book's content. Still others prefer a more thorough overview. If you prefer a brief overview, read on. If you wish to skip the overview and head immediately and directly to the content of the book, go to *Lesson One: Healthcare Organization Business Processes and Management* or to *Lesson One Content and Discussion*. If you prefer a more detailed overview at this time, please see *Appendix A: Expanded Book Overview*. Appendix A is redundant with the information contained in this section. It is provided because some readers prefer a more detailed overview of the book than is provided in this section. The Table of Contents follows this brief overview section.

*****

Have you ever needed to resolve a billing or other issue with a healthcare organization and thought that there must be a better, more efficient and more customer-friendly way to operate such a business process? For example, have you thought that there should be an easier way to read your bill or pay your bill? Or do you work in a healthcare organization and find yourself thinking that there must be better ways for the business processes to function? If you have, this book is for you.

This book is an overview of healthcare organization business processes including business process management approaches as well as a discussion of healthcare organization entrepreneurship as a business process. This book is for you if you are interested in the world of business processes and business process management in healthcare organizations in the United States.

This book is for those with a developing interest in healthcare organization operations as they pertain to business processes and their management. It is also suitable for those who have some expertise, but who wish an overview or refresher of these topics.

Unlike most other texts, this book has an agenda or purpose aimed at aiding the reader. The book knows that you have your own specific personal goals regarding business processes in healthcare organizations (e.g., improve your ability to facilitate the management of business processes in a healthcare organization, improve your healthcare administration skills, learn more about business processes in healthcare organizations in general). The purpose of this book is to enable you to develop your own learning path to reach your learning goal regardless of what that goal happens to be. The intent of the book is to provide you with content and resources to pursue a personal learning path. That content extends past the reading of this text and will help you in your chosen work or study.

The unique purpose of the book requires a unique format. The format includes tons of resources (some would say encyclopedic) coupled with the Socratic Method and suggested competency development tasks. The Socratic Method promotes understanding of a topic by posing questions on that topic. Answering the question requires a learner/reader to think critically and synthesize information. The overall competency goal for all readers of this book is that it enables each reader to think more critically and more independently about business processes in healthcare organizations.

The book is organized into four (4) lessons. Each lesson is organized around competency objectives, questions, readings, competency development tasks (e.g., quiz) to organize your thinking and cement your learning. It is a format which makes extensive use of the resources available on the internet. As such the book provides links to external sites to connect you to the larger "*real world*" of healthcare organizations to help you better build your own learning path. The links also serve as resources you can use after you complete this book. Many might say that that the most valuable part of this book is the list of resources provided for the reader.

These links (more than 550) are directly accessible in the content in the e-book version. For the print version – and for reference in the e-book version – the full URL for each link in the book can be found at the corresponding in-text link number [bib#] in the section at the end of the book entitled *Bibliography: Associated URL/Link List*. The list includes data, management, and research links needed for healthcare administration, management, and operations related to business processes in a healthcare organization.

The competency development tasks in this book facilitate content mastery to help you organize your thinking. Such organized thought should help you determine the relationship between the book content, a personal learning path, and achievement of personal goals. Competency development tasks in this book are: discussion questions, quizzes, and a project. Again, this is a Socratic approach in that the book asks for your thinking on the topics.

The included suggested project is intended to help you synthesize content material by developing business processes for a healthcare organization of your choice the way you would have things run in the best of all worlds. The suggested design format to communicate these business processes is an electronic memo format. An example of a completed memo project is found in *Appendix B: Memo Example*. The memo is an artifact which you can circulate to colleagues or use as the basis for a talk or presentation event. The philosophy behind this project is that more learning occurs – and learning is more fun – if you can actually build/create something from the content and it is useful beyond the reading of this book.

And because everyone loves a road trip/field trip, there are also "*virtual field trips*" to the often hidden places of interest on the web. There are also trivia questions – just for fun – because everyone also loves little known, but interesting, fun facts.

This book is dense in the physics sense of the word. There is a lot of detail we have to introduce to get people on the playing field. There is no royal road to acquiring that depth of information. We have attempted to organize the information and to make it searchable. One needs to take a break every so often to absorb the material. This is one of the reasons why virtual field trips and trivia questions are provided. Historical and social context is important in healthcare. Many of the links, virtual field trips, and trivia questions provide this context.

This book follows the content of and can be used as an adjunct to the Coursera course: *Business Process Management in Healthcare Organizations* found at https://www.coursera.org/learn/business-process-management-in-healthcare-organizations. Should you prefer a learning experience which can result in an earned certificate or prefer a community of learners in the same course of study, consider enrolling in the Coursera course.

Note: *The photograph shown at the beginning of this section is by rawpixel and was downloaded from Unsplash (https://unsplash.com/). The photographs used for the cover of the book were produced by Mesh, Tom Grimbert, and rawpixel (downloaded from Unsplash).*

ISBN-13: 978-1-7336928-4-7
Imprint: Margaret Kilduff, Independent Publishing
Version 1.0, June 2020
Text copyright © 2020
All Rights Reserved
Margaret Kilduff, Ph.D.
Professor Emerita
Rutgers University

Table of Contents

Lesson Three (L3): Healthcare Organization Electronic Patient/Customer Records Business Processes 99

Lesson One (L1): Healthcare Organization Business Processes and Management

Note: The above picture is adapted from the one by Christina @ wocintechchat.com found on Unsplash
(https://unsplash.com/photos/0Nfqp0WiJqc)

L1 Competency Objective

This lesson provides an overview of the course as well as an overview of healthcare organization business processes and business process management.

- Define healthcare organization business processes and business process management

L1 Getting Started

L1 Welcome and Find Your Seat

The start of every learning path – the start of every course, every lesson, every targeted learning adventure – begins by "*finding your seat*". It begins by finding the location best suited for you to study and learn the targeted material. In today's world – in today's online information world – that "*seat*" can be in your kitchen, a coffee shop, on public transportation – anywhere there is an internet connection.

There is something nice, however, about finding a seat – even if only in your mind's eye – in a library, especially one of the iconic libraries. Such iconic libraries are architecturally stunning and provide a wonderful environment in which to ponder, consider, and learn. A few are shown below. Feel free to "*take a seat*" – any seat – in your mind's eye in one of them before moving on to the next sections.

Fisher Fine Arts Library, University of Pennsylvania [bib#1] (founded in 1888)

Image from Wikipedia, File:Furness Lib interior looking N UPenn.JPG [bib#2]

Suzzallo Library, University of Washington [bib#3] (founded in 1926)

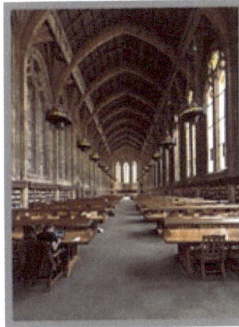

Image from Wikipedia, File:MK03235 University of Washington Suzzallo Library.jpg [bib#4]

William W. Cook Legal Research Library, University of Michigan [bib#5] (founded in 1931)

Image from Wikipedia, File:UniversityofMichiganLawLibrary.jpg [bib#6]

L1 Discussion Question: Personal Learning Goal for this Learning Path

After finding your seat, it is often helpful to consider your personal learning goal for a learning path. Almost everyone has a personal learning goal at the beginning of every book, every course, every lesson, and every targeted learning adventure. Do you have a personal learning goal for this book? If so, what is it? Where do you want to be at the end of the learning path defined by this book? Where does this book fit into your personally chosen learning path which leads to achievement of personal goals?

L1 Content and Discussion

This lesson provides an overview of business processes and management in healthcare organizations. Upon successful completion of this lesson, you will be able to: define healthcare organization business processes and business process management. There are topic questions, a discussion question, a quiz, a trivia question, and a field trip. The lesson should take 4 - 6 hours of work to successfully complete. There are also videos which provide supplemental content which can help you better define your personal learning path. There are many wonderful videos in the public domain which are relevant to the topics in this book. One is listed immediately below.

*****

> *Video* [bib#7]: *There are many wonderful videos in the public domain which are relevant to the topics in this book. One such video –* **Kenn Borek Air's South Pole Rescue Team - 2017 National Air and Space Museum Trophy Winner** *– is a YouTube video produced by the Smithsonian. This video provides an overview of the successful rescue of two ill researchers from the NSF's Amundsen-Scott South Pole Station in Antarctica. The link for the video is:*
> https://www.youtube.com/watch?v=XGc-o1ufjjY

*****

This lesson addresses five (5) topics organized as questions. The questions/topics for Lesson One are:

1. What is the general definition of healthcare organization business processes?

2. What is healthcare organization business process management?

3. What are healthcare organization operational business processes?

4. What are healthcare organization supporting business processes?

5. What are healthcare organization management business processes?

L1 Topic 1 (T1). What is the general definition of healthcare organization business processes?

Healthcare organization business processes are those business processes common to all healthcare organizations. This section addresses:

- Business Process General Definition and Categories
- Difference Between a Business Process, Workflow, and Checklist
- Use Case Definition

L1-T1. Business Process General Definition and Categories

There is no one universally accepted precise definition of a business process. Business Dictionary [bib#8], for example, defines a business process as a:

"series of logically related activities or tasks (such as planning, production, or sales) performed together to produce a defined set of results".

The Business Process Management Glossary [bib#9] states that a:

"business process must have clearly defined inputs and outputs. Inputs make up all of the contributions for a product or service".

The American College of Healthcare Executives (ACHE) [bib#10] defines business processes as the processes which pertain to *"specific areas/concepts of the organization*". However, there is a similarity across all definitions. In general, a business process is a series of actions completed to achieve a specified organizational objective or goal.

Adam Smith [bib#11] is credited with conceptualizing the idea of a business process in Chapter One, Page 3 of his 1776 publication *An Inquiry into the Nature and Causes of the Wealth of Nations*. In this publication, which is often referred to as the *Wealth of Nations* [bib#12], Smith conceptualizes the production of a pin as a process:

> "*One man draws out the wire; another straights it; a third cuts it; a fourth points it; a fifth grinds it at the top for receiving the head; to make the head requires two or three distinct operations; to put it on is a peculiar business; to whiten the pins is another; it is even a trade by itself to put them into the paper; and the important business of making a pin is, in this manner, divided into about eighteen distinct operations, which, in some manufactories, are all performed by distinct hands, though in others the same man will sometimes perform two or three of them.*"

In general, business processes are organized into three categories: operational business processes, supporting business processes, and management business processes.

- Operational Business Processes (sometimes called Core Business Processes or Primary Business Processes) are the processes which produce direct value for the customer; they produce the organization's product and often have direct contact with the organization's customer. In a healthcare organization, these processes are those related to health care delivery.

- Supporting Business Processes (sometimes called Secondary Business Processes) support the Operational Business Processes. They are the "back office" functions which do not usually have direct contact with customers. Examples of Supporting Business Processes in healthcare organizations – and in all organizations – are those related to human resources, facilities, and financial management.

- Management Business Processes regulate and control the Operational Business Processes and the Supporting Business Processes. They do not usually have direct contact with customers. Examples of Management Business Processes in healthcare organizations – and in all organizations – are those related to governance, quality assurance, and strategic planning.

Usually an organization's business processes affect only the organization. However, sometimes that business process has a far-reaching societal impact. Such was the case of Railway Time [bib#13] in the United States which led to Standard Time [bib#14] and Daylight Saving Time [bib#15].

It all began on August 12, 1853 when two trains from the Providence and Worcester Railroad collided head-on [bib#16] in Pawtucket, Rhode Island killing 14 and injuring more than 40. The two trains collided because the official time for each train (the train conductor's watch) was not synchronized. The time on each conductor's watch was not the same.

There was an official train schedule and according to the schedule, one train was to be off the single track and on a double track at a specific time. The trains were to pass each other on the double track and, clearly, not collide on the single track. According to one conductor's watch – the other train was on the double track according to schedule. Unfortunately, the watch for the other conductor was set to a different time and his train was running on schedule on the single track.

This accident motivated the Providence and Worcester Railroad to develop a new business process – to synchronize all station clocks and conductor watches – known as Railway Time. The first use of Railway Time in the world was by the Great Western Railway in England which synchronized all of its organizational clocks and watches in 1840 with Greenwich Mean Time (GMT) [bib#17]; the time in London.

Other American railroads followed the example of the Providence and Worcester Railroad with their own Railway Time; that is, the Railway Time for each railroad was not necessarily synchronized with any other railroad. Nor was Railway Time necessarily the time recognized in the towns and areas through which the railroad traveled. The norm and tradition until the late 1800s in the United States was for each local area to set its own local time based largely on a local sundial (solar time [bib#18]) sometimes called local mean time [bib#19].

In 1870, Charles Dowd [bib#20] published *A System of National Times for Railroads* which suggested that all railroads in the United States use one Railway Time (all railroads synchronize all organizational clocks and watches to the same time). There was little enthusiasm for his suggestion, but it did lead to William F. Allen's proposal [bib#21] of Standard Railway Time where Railway Time was divided into five geographic time zones and all railroads within one time zone were to use the same Railway Time.

This was implemented on November 18, 1883 [bib#22] upon on a telegraph signal from the Allegheny Observatory in Pittsburgh. By and large local communities within each of the time zones adopted the local Railway Time as local time. There was no requirement for them to do so, but most communities did.

However, the Standard Time Act of 1918 [bib#23] officially established Railway Standard Time (now called Standard Time) as the law of the land. The Interstate Commerce Commission (ICC) has jurisdiction over [bib#24] the time zone boundaries. This Act also outlined the use of Daylight Saving Time, but that mandate was dropped after a year because of great opposition.

The use of Daylight Saving Time was a voluntary local issue until World War II. After WWII, Daylight Saving Time returned to its voluntary local jurisdiction. The Uniform Time Act of 1966 [bib#25] established national standards for Daylight Saving Time, but allowed states to decide whether to implement Daylight Saving Time or not. Hawaii and most of Arizona, for example, do not now use Daylight Saving Time.

*****

*****

L1-T1. Difference Between a Business Process, Workflow, Checklist, and Use Case

Many people use the term workflow and business process interchangeably, but many people also define a difference between the terms. For those who define a difference:

- A workflow is the steps/activities needed to successfully complete a specific task (micro-level step-by-step instructions to complete a task).

- A business process is the activities and resources needed to successfully achieve an organizational objective or goal (more macro level); a workflow can be part of a business process.

For example, a business process document usually contains (at a minimum):

- Process Purpose (e.g., to ensure that the healthcare organization has a sufficient number and distribution of appropriately credentialed personnel for health care delivery)

- Process Input (e.g., the process is initiated upon official notification to human resources that there is a need for credentialed personnel for health care delivery)

- <u>Process Flow</u> (e.g., First Step. Send a personnel hire form to the appropriate person to complete to gather details of the specific personnel requirements..... Last Step. Send the selected candidate an offer of employment)

- <u>Process Output</u> (e.g., a person who meets the specific personnel requirements accepts an offer of employment from human resources)

The Process Flow is a workflow. So a business process is more than a workflow and may contain one or more workflows.

A checklist is a summary of the completed activities - not a workflow. Sometimes the checklist can be ordered in an efficient workflow manner, but it does not have to be in order to be a checklist. A good example is a grocery list. Your grocery list may list (in the following order): eggs, apples, coffee, milk, and lettuce. As you put each item in your cart, you usually mark the item off your list. But you do not usually pick up the items in the checklist order. For example, eggs and milk are usually located near each other as are apples and lettuce. Just after you pick up the eggs, you probably pick up the milk even though applies are listed next.

Using a checklist as a workflow may not be harmful when grocery shopping (you just spend extra time walking from the eggs to the apples to the coffee and then back near the eggs to get the milk and then back near the apples to get the lettuce), but it can be harmful if time is of the essence.

For example, a pilot may have a checklist to use in an aviation emergency. If the checklist is not ordered in the most efficient workflow [bib#28] for that emergency, time lost following the inefficient workflow checklist may mean the emergency is not resolved safely.

The aviation industry is well-known for using checklists to improve safety. Particularly well-known is the pre-flight checklist [bib#29] used by pilots to ensure that everything is set for a safe take-off. This checklist resulted from the October 30, 1935 crash [bib#30] of a "*Boeing Model 299 Flying Fortress, NX13372 – the most technologically sophisticated airplane of its time*" shortly after take-off.

It was determined that the crash was caused by the failure of the pilots to perform a routine function – release the flight control gust locks – while on the ground. Aviation experts decided that planes had become so complex that it was no longer possible for pilots to rely on memory alone for the pre-flight tasks. A reminder in the form of a checklist was needed and the pre-flight checklist became a cockpit safety standard.

Some argue checklists can be as helpful in the healthcare industry to improve safety as they are in the aviation industry. Two of the more famous checklists in health care delivery are the World Health Organization (WHO) Surgical Safety Checklist [bib#31] and the Keystone ICU Project [bib#32] checklist which was spearheaded by Peter J. Pronovost [bib#33] to reduce the number of catheter-related bloodstream infections [bib#34] in the intensive care unit (ICU). The WHO checklist contains 19 items divided into three categories/timeframes:

1. Before induction of anesthesia;
2. Before skin incision; and
3. Before patient leaves operating room.

The Keystone checklist contains 5 items for clinicians in the ICU to do with respect to patient catheters:

1. Wash their hands with soap;
2. Clean the patient's skin with chlorhexidine antiseptic;
3. Put sterile drapes over the entire patient;
4. Wear a sterile mask, hat, gown and gloves; and
5. Put a sterile dressing over the catheter site.

The impact of the use of these two (and other) checklists [bib#35] on patient morbidity and mortality has been mixed. Some studies report vast improvements [bib#36] in patient safety (improvements in patient morbidity and mortality) and others report no difference. Some have concluded that healthcare checklists may improve safety when:

*"processes that are simple, easy to follow, standardised and (perhaps) time critica*l ... *Overreliance on checklists as a safety net*

can lead to omission of other safety practices that may better support safety through reliability and resilience" (Website Source of Quote1 [bib#37]).

"Checklists are a remarkably useful tool in improving safety, but they are not a panacea. As checklists have been more widely implemented, it has become clear that their success depends on appropriately targeting the intervention and utilizing a careful implementation strategy" (Website Source of Quote2 [bib#38]).

L1-T1. Use Case Definition

Use Case [bib#39] is a term usually associated with software development. A Use Case describes how the end user interacts with (views and uses) the software application. It describes the end user requirements for using the system (what features does the end user want). A Use Case provides a framework for the software developer regarding what the software is supposed to do. A Use Case does not typically include the software workflow.

If a business process is automated, a Use Case describes how the end user interacts with (views and uses) the business process software application. And there are usually multiple categories of end users with different requirements (want different features). For example, employees in an organization's payroll office responsible for producing the payroll want uses (views, features) to be able to efficiently and effectively generate the payroll for all of the organization's employees. Any individual employee only wants uses (views, features) of that same payroll system pertaining to the individual employee's payments from the organization.

The U.S. Department of Health and Human Services (HHS) usability.gov [bib#40]website provides guidance for those developing government websites to inform the public and defines a website use case [bib#41] as a:

"written description of how users will perform tasks on your website. It outlines, from a user's point of view, a system's behavior as it

responds to a request. Each use case is represented as a sequence of simple steps, beginning with a user's goal and ending when that goal is fulfilled."

The Use Case concept can be applied to a patient-centered healthcare organization's business processes regardless of whether the processes are automated. Such a Use Case describes how the patient/customer interacts with (views and uses) the healthcare organization's business processes. It describes the patient/customer requirements for doing business with the healthcare organization (what features does the patient/customer want). A Use Case provides a framework for the healthcare organization what the business processes are supposed to do (Use Case Business Process Management).

For example, a simple Use Case for a patient/customer picking up a prescription from a retail pharmacy might be:

Step 1. Easily enter an appealing store with the retail pharmacy;

Step 2. Stand in an easy-to-find and organized line at the prescription pick-up counter;

Step 3. Receive the correct prescription and easily pay for it;

Step 4. Easily leave the store.

Not listed in this Use Case scenario are the business processes used by the retail pharmacy to make this patient/customer experience possible (e.g., business processes which produce an appealing store space, an organized prescription pickup line, a quality and accurate prescription, and prescription payment processing).

L1 Topic 2 (T2). What is healthcare organization business process management?

As a general rule, Business Process Management (BPM) focuses on improving organization performance and outcomes through efficient and effective management of the organization's business processes. Often the focus is on automating these processes for the purpose of improving them.

This section address:

- Business Process Management (BPM) Definition
- Business Process Documentation and Templates
- Use Case Documentation and Templates
- Visualization, Notation, and Tools

L1-T2. Business Process Management (BPM) Definition

Although there is general agreement on the general focus of BPM, there is no general agreement on a precise definition of BPM. However, a commonly used definition [bib#42] is that:

"*Business Process Management (BPM) is a discipline involving any combination of modeling, automation, execution, control, measurement and optimization of business activity flows, in support of enterprise goals, spanning systems, employees, customers and partners within and beyond the enterprise boundaries.*"

The Business Process Management Institute (BPMInstitute) defines BPM [bib#43]:

"*as the definition, improvement and management of a firm's end-to-end enterprise business processes in order to achieve three outcomes crucial to a performance-based, customer-driven firm: 1) clarity on strategic direction, 2) alignment of the firm's resources, and 3) increased discipline in daily operations.*"

BPMInstitute [bib#44] "*is the largest practitioner-led community of BPM professionals in the world, with over 50,000 members*". The Institute offers a number of certificates [bib#45] including the Business Process Management Professional (BPMP) certificate [bib#46] .

The Association of Business Process Management Professionals (ABPMP) International defines BPM [bib#47] as:

> "*a disciplined approach to identify, design, execute, document, measure, monitor, and control both automated and non-automated business processes to achieve consistent, targeted results aligned with an organization's strategic goals.*
>
> *BPM involves the deliberate, collaborative and increasingly technology-aided definition, improvement, innovation, and management of end-to-end business processes that drive business results, create value, and enable an organization to meet its business objectives with more agility.*
>
> *BPM enables an enterprise to align its business processes to its business strategy, leading to effective overall company performance through improvements of specific work activities either within a specific department, across the enterprise, or between organizations.*"

ABPMP International [bib#48]

> "*is the non-profit professional association dedicated to the field of Business Process Management. Through a global network, ABPMP connects over 15,000+ individuals representing more than 750 corporations and 56 chapters worldwide.*"

ABPMP offers a number of certificates [bib#49] including the Certified Business Process Professional (CBPP) certificate [bib#50].

Besides the BPMInstitute and ABPMP International, two other professional resources for those interested in Business Process Management (BPM) are:

- BPM.com [bib#51] which is "*the Internet's leading destination for articles, news, research and white papers on Business Process Management, Process Modeling, Business Rules, and Case Management*".

- [Workflow Management Coalition (WfMC)](#) [bib#52] which is "*a global organization of adopters, developers, consultants, analysts, as well as university and research groups engaged in workflow and BPM. The WfMC creates and contributes to process related standards, educates the market on related issues, and is the only standards organization that concentrates purely on process.*"

L1-T2. Business Process Documentation and Templates

A basic part of Business Process Management is the documentation of business processes. Just as there is no one universally accepted precise definition of a business process or business process management, there is no one universally accepted template for what business process document should contain. In Topic 1, it was stated that a business process document usually contains (at a minimum):

- Process Purpose
- Process Input
- Process Flow (The Process Flow is a workflow. So a business process is more than a workflow and may contain one or more workflows).
- Process Output

However, a complete business process document usually contains (not necessarily in the following order):

1. Process Name: A unique name which quickly identifies the process

2. Process Purpose: A brief statement on this business process' role in achieving an organizational objective or goal

3. Process Scope: A brief statement of the activities covered by this process (e.g., only internal communications not external communications)

4. Process Input: A brief statement on when this process is activated; the starting/trigger point for this process

5. Process Boundaries: A brief statement on when the process begins and ends; for example, the process input may not be part of the process, but begins immediately thereafter (those responsible for the process are not responsible for making sure that they get the process input)

6. Process Flow: A detailed sequential list of steps/instructions to complete the process; sometimes documented as a list of steps/instructions and sometimes documented visually in a flow diagram; a workflow, so a business process is more than a workflow and may contain one or more workflows

7. Process Output: A brief statement on when this process ends; the tangible result/outcome produced by this process which may serve as the input to another process

8. Exceptions to the Normal Process Flow: A brief statement on what happens if the Process Flow steps cannot be completed (e.g., the process ends and the Process Input is revised)

9. Control Points and Measurements: A brief statement as to which steps measurements will be taken and used as control points evaluated against benchmarks to be used for organizational re-evaluation (e.g., a step which requires the review of qualified applicants for a job finds that the measure for that step is 0 – no qualified applicants applied – which serves as a control point to activate a review of why the number of applicants is 0 and discussion of what the organization can do to increase the number of qualified applicants)

10. Roles and Responsibilities: A brief statement and list of the job titles responsible for implementing each step and any decision-making associated with the steps and process

11. Process Approval: A brief statement on the method for reviewing, revising, and approving the process itself and the process documents as well as the date the process and any revisions were approved

Healthcare organizations (all organizations) should not only document business processes, but also document the existence of all business processes; there should be a complete inventory of all business processes and their associated documents.

There are a number of business process document templates available without cost which can make the development of a business process and document easier. Some of these are:

- Project Management Docs, Business Process Document [bib#53] website

- smartsheet, Free Process Document Templates [bib#54] website

- Intelivate, Process Documentation – Protecting the Lifeline of Your Business Operations (Includes Process Templates) [bib#55] website which includes not just business process templates, but also a description of methods and templates used to create an inventory of business processes

- TEMPLATE.NET, 13+ Business Process Examples [bib#56] website

- Creately Blog, What is Process Documentation - The Easy Guide to Process Documentation [bib#57] website

L1-T2. Use Case Documentation and Templates

Just as there is no one universally accepted template for what a business process document should contain, there is no one universally accepted template for a Use Case document. However, in general a Use Case document (which is very similar to a business process document) contains:

- Use Case Name: A unique name which quickly identifies the use case (similar to the Process Name)

- <u>Use Case Brief Description</u>:   A brief statement of the broad scope of the use case. Examples for a Use Case for healthcare organization business processes include the patient/customer perspective on: a routine dental checkup for a new patient/customer, the experience of short term inpatient admitted for elective surgery, customer pickup of an ongoing prescription at a retail pharmacy (similar to the Process Purpose and Process Scope)

- <u>Use Case Actors</u>: A brief statement or list of the types of users who will be part of this use (who can participate in the activities described in the use case). Examples for a healthcare organization include patients/customers and their families (similar to, but the opposite of, Process Roles and Responsibilities)

- <u>Use Case Preconditions</u>: A brief statement of anything that can be assumed to be true when the use case begins. Examples for a healthcare organization might include: the patient/customer has made an appointment and completed the initial visit paperwork, the patient/customer has been evaluated and recommended for elective surgery prior to arrival at the inpatient facility, the customer at the retail pharmacy knows that the prescription is ready for pickup (similar to Process Input and Boundaries).

- <u>Use Case Basic Flow</u>: A brief statement on the set of steps the actors take to accomplish the goal of the use case and a clear description of the system's response to each actor step. For a healthcare organization, it would be the steps patients/customers take to achieve their goals and the healthcare organization's business process response to each step. For example, a patient/customer enters a dental office (actor step) and is immediately greeted by dental office personnel (healthcare organization response) (similar to Process Flow).

- <u>Use Case Alternate and Exception Flow</u>: A brief statement on what happens if the Use Case Basic Flow steps cannot be completed as specified (e.g., if, for some reason, dental office personnel are not present to greet the patient/customer, the patient/customer is directed via a sign to press a buzzer).

There are a number of use case document templates available without cost which can make the development of a use case document easier. Some examples are the templates found at the 40 Use Case Templates & Examples (Word, PDF) [bib#58] website.

L1-T2. Visualization, Notation, and Tools

It is often helpful to visualize the business process as a whole, the Process Flow workflow steps, and the use case as a whole. The activity to transform the written business process document into a graphical visualization is called Business Process Mapping. So useful is this visualization that standards for this graphical display exist.

These standards are called Business Process Model and Notation (BPMN [bib#59]). BPMN was developed by the Business Process Management Initiative (BPMI) in 2000 which merged with and became the Object Management Group [bib#60] in 2005. The current standards can be found at The Object Management Group Business Process Model and Notation (OMG-BPMN [bib#61]) website. The graphical display is sometimes called a Business Process Diagram (BPD) or Business Process Map.

These business process visualizations look like flowcharts. And the same flowchart design features can be used to visualize the Process Flow workflow steps, and the use case as a whole.

There are a number of software flowchart tools to help in development of visualization. One is Microsoft Visio [bib#62]. You can also use most word processing software to create a flowchart, but it is a little more involved and cumbersome to do so than using software designed for flowchart development. There is a charge for using Visio, but there are free alternatives to Visio [bib#63], including free alternatives for use with Mac and Linux. These include, but are not limited to:

- Lucidchart [bib#64]
- Creately [bib#65]
- LibreOffice Draw [bib#66]

*****

> **Video** [bib#67]: *The video for Topic 2 –* **How to Create Flowcharts Using LibreOffice Draw**– *is a YouTube video produced by DCP Web Designers. This video demonstrates how to create flowcharts using LibreOffice Draw. The link for the video is:*
> https://www.youtube.com/watch?v=JHnUZLyPoUw

*****

A good description of flowchart development can also be found the Flowcharting Medical Processes - Research [bib#68] website. There are also websites which have templates and additional information for flowcharts for varying purposes. Some of these are:

- Edraw, Free Workflow Diagram Templates for Word, PowerPoint, PDF [bib#69]
- TEMPLATE.NET, 20+ Workflow Diagram Templates – Sample, Example, Format Download [bib#70]
- Lucidchart, Flowchart Examples and Templates [bib#71]
- Creately, Flowchart Templates & Examples - Download for Free [bib#72]
- All About Business Process Mapping, Flow Charts and Diagrams [bib#73]
- Step-By-Step Guide to Business Process Mapping [bib#74]
- Smartdraw, Business Process Map [bib#75]
- Essential Guide to Business Process Mapping [bib#76]
- use case diagram (UML use case diagram) [bib#77]
- Process Flowchart VS Use Case Diagram [bib#78]
- BPMN Tutorial: Quick-Start Guide to Business Process Model and Notation [bib#79]
- BPMN & BPMN 2.0 Tutorial [bib#80]
- Process mapping as a framework for performance improvement in emergency general surgery [bib#81]

L1 Topic 3 (T3). What are healthcare organization operational business processes?

Operational Business Processes (sometimes called Core Business Processes or Primary Business Processes) are the processes which produce direct value for the customer; they produce the organization's product and often have direct contact with the organization's customer. In a healthcare organization, these processes are those related to health care delivery.

Each healthcare organization has its own unique set of operational business processes. However, there are some commonalities across all healthcare organizations. Regardless of healthcare organization type (e.g., inpatient short-term, inpatient long-term, outpatient), the operational business process categories can be divided into three general categories: Patient/Customer Intake, Health Care Delivery, and Patient/Customer Discharge.

For the purposes of this book, the entire eleven (11) item business process list shown in Topic 2 will not illustrated and discussed for Supporting Business Processes. Only four (4) items will be discussed:

- Process Purpose (List Item 2)
- Process Input (List Item 4)
- Process Flow (List Item 6)
- Process Output (List Item 7)

The specifics of each of these four items (and, indeed, the specifics of all eleven items) will differ by healthcare organization. There is no one description of each of these items which is suitable for every healthcare organization.

This section addresses:

- Patient/Customer Intake Business Processes
- Health Care Delivery Business Processes
- Patient/Customer Discharge Business Processes

L1-T3. Patient/Customer Intake Business Processes

For inpatient healthcare organizations (short-term and long-term), the Patient/Customer Intake Business Processes are usually called Admissions Processes. There is no such common term for outpatient healthcare organizations. These processes do not pertain to those related to people asking for information about the healthcare organization. The Patient/Customer Intake Business Processes may be different for:

- "New" patients/customers (ones who have never before received health care delivery services from the healthcare organization) versus "prior" patients/customers (ones who have received health care delivery services from the organization at a prior time).

- Those patients/customers with a scheduled appointment for specific health care delivery services versus those without an appointment for health care delivery

Process Purpose: In general, it is to ensure that the healthcare organization has the information needed to efficiently and effectively deliver health care to the patient/customer.

- Such information often includes: patient identifying and demographic information (e.g., name, address, birth date), patient insurance information, and patient medical information (e.g., allergies).

Process Input: In general, the process is initiated when the patient/customer arrives at the healthcare organization and contacts the organizational personnel charged with check in tasks.

- Who this is will vary by organization. In retail pharmacies, this person is often the pharmacist at the prescription pickup counter. In a dental office or physician office, it is often the office receptionist. In emergency rooms, urgent care facilities, hospitals, and nursing homes, it is often people in the Admitting or Admissions Department.

Process Flow: The general steps are: 1) Greet the patient/customer; 2) Collect the required information from the patient/customer; and 3) Notify the health care delivery team that the patient/customer has completed the intake business process and is waiting to begin the delivery of health care (e.g., the patient/customer has arrived and is in the waiting area). The specifics will vary by healthcare organization.

- An example of visualization for this Process Flow can be found at the Creately, Patient Check in Process [bib#82] website.

- Another example can be found at the Agency for Healthcare Research and Quality (AHRQ), Health Information Technology, Flowchart [bib#83] website, specifically the Patient Check-In Flowchart [bib#84].

Process Output: In general, the process ends when the healthcare organization begins health care delivery to the patient/customer.

- In retail pharmacies, this will be when the pharmacist goes to get the ordered prescription. In a dental office, physician office, emergency rooms, urgent care facilities, hospitals, and nursing homes, it will be when the patient leaves any waiting area to go to the health care delivery room.

L1-T3. Health Care Delivery Business Processes

Health Care Delivery Business Processes are those which deliver health care. These will differ by type of healthcare organization and the Process Flow will differ for the various healthcare needs of the patient/customer.

Process Purpose: In general, it is to ensure that the healthcare organization delivers the highest quality health care efficiently and effectively to the patient/customer.

Process Input: In general, the process is initiated when a health care delivery professional begins to interact with the patient/customer for the purpose of health care delivery.

- In retail pharmacies, health care delivery usually starts when the pharmacist goes to retrieve the patient's/customer's prescription. It should be noted that if the prescription is ready for pickup that much work in a different business process was done to prepare the prescription before the patient/customer arrived. In a dental office or physician office, health care delivery usually starts when a health care professional meets the patient/customer in the waiting area to be escorted to a health care delivery area (e.g., examination room).

Process Flow: The steps will vary greatly by type of healthcare organization and the specific health needs of the patient/customer. Examples of visualizations of various Process Flows can be found at the:

- Agency for Healthcare Research and Quality (AHRQ), Emergency Department Workflow Diagrams [bib#85]

- Agency for Healthcare Research and Quality (AHRQ), Primary Care Workflow Diagrams [bib#86]

- AHRQ, Health Information Technology, Flowchart [bib#83] website, specifically the Common Office Visit Flowchart [bib#87], Nurse-Only Visit Flowchart [bib#88], and the Physician Assistant (PA) Office Visit Flowchart [bib#89].

Within the general health care delivery flowchart are more detailed steps/flowcharts related to the specific health care the patient/customer receives. Examples include those found at the Medicine Today, Clinical Flowcharts [bib#90] website as well as the In-Office Prescribing Flowchart - Paper System [bib#91] found at the AHRQ, Health Information Technology, Flowchart [bib#83] website.

Process Output: In general, the process ends when the health care delivery professional ends the interaction with the patient/customer for the purpose of health care delivery.

- In retail pharmacies, health care delivery usually ends when the pharmacist has given the prescription to the patient/customer, verified that the prescription is correct, and answered any questions the patient/customer has about the prescription. In a dental office or physician office, health care delivery usually ends when a health care professional escorts the patient/customer from the health care delivery area to the waiting area.

Key components of health care delivery are the business processes related to surgery. Approximately 50 million inpatient surgical procedures [bib#92] are done each year in the United States. William Stewart Halsted [bib#93] (1852 - 1922) is generally considered to be the "Father of Modern Surgery". He was the Johns Hopkins University School of Medicine's [bib#94] (established 1893):

"first professor of surgery and surgeon in chief at The Johns Hopkins Hospital, William Halsted is known for exemplary skill as a diagnostician and an advocate of anti-infection surgical techniques. He revolutionizes surgical practice by insisting on antiseptic methods, including the pioneering use of rubber gloves, gentle handling of tissues, and the use of small, fine silk sutures" (Website Source of Quote3 [bib#95]).

*****

Video [bib#96]: *The video for Topic 3 – **How it Works: Bloodless Medicine and Surgery, An Alternative to Blood Transfusion** – is a YouTube video produced by Johns Hopkins Medicine. This video is an overview of bloodless medicine and surgery as an alternative to blood transfusion. The link for the video is:*
https://www.youtube.com/watch?v=LmBX55IlAzg

*****

The Johns Hopkins University School of Medicine was also the first to have a medical illustration program – founded in 1911 as the Hopkins Department of Art as Applied to Medicine [bib#97]. The Department's first chairperson was Max Broedel [bib#98] who is generally considered to be the

"Father of Modern Medical Illustration". "*Copying is not medical illustrating,*" Broedel said:

> "*In a medical drawing, full comprehension must precede execution.*" He "*always aimed to draw a picture that would show more than any photograph could. This required an exquisite understanding of anatomy that could be gained only by dissection or watching surgery.*" (Website Source of Quote4 [bib#99]).

L1-T3. Patient/Customer Discharge Business Processes

For inpatient healthcare organizations (short-term and long-term), the Patient/Customer Discharge Business Processes are usually very structured and formal with specific people assigned with the tasks. The process is usually a little less structured and formal for outpatient healthcare organizations.

Process Purpose: In general, it is to ensure that the healthcare organization formally ends and resolves the specific health care delivery to a specific patient/customer.

Process Input: In general, the process is initiated when the patient/customer arrives in the waiting or general non-health care delivery section of the healthcare organization after health care has been delivered.

- In retail pharmacies, this process is usually completed by the pharmacist after delivering the prescription to the patient/customer who processes payment for the prescription from the patient/customer. In a dental office or physician office, the office receptionist often finalizes payment and next appointment details when the patient/customer enters the waiting area. In emergency rooms, urgent care facilities, hospitals, and nursing homes, the tasks are usually the responsibility of people in a Patient Discharge Department.

Process Flow: The general steps are: 1) Greet the patient/customer; and 2) Collect any required payment and resolve any healthcare organization details (e.g., make a follow-up appointment, confirm the patient's/customer's discharge plans and location).the required information from the patient/customer. The specifics will vary by healthcare organization.

- An example of a visualization for this Process Flow can be found at the Agency for Healthcare Research and Quality (AHRQ), Health Information Technology, Flowchart [bib#83] website, specifically the Patient Check-Out Flowchart [bib#100] which is attached below.

Process Output: In general, the process ends when the patient/customer leaves the healthcare organization.

- In retail pharmacies, this will be when the patient/customer leaves the pharmacy counter. In a dental office, physician office, emergency rooms, urgent care facilities, hospitals, and nursing homes, it will be when the patient/customer leaves the healthcare organization building.

L1 Topic 4 (T4). What are healthcare organization supporting business processes?

Supporting Business Processes (sometimes called Secondary Business Processes) support the Operational Business Processes. They are the "back office" functions which do not usually have direct contact with customers. Examples of Supporting Business Processes in healthcare organizations - and in all organizations - are those related to human resources, facilities, and financial management.

Each healthcare organization has its own unique set of supporting business processes. However, there are some commonalities across all healthcare organizations. Regardless of healthcare organization type (e.g., inpatient short-term, inpatient long-term, outpatient), two of the most important supporting business process categories are Human Resources Management and Financial Management. Only these two are addressed in this section.

This section addresses:

- Healthcare Organization Human Resources Management Business Processes
- Healthcare Organization Financial Management Business Processes

As with the Operational Business Processes, for the purposes of this book, the entire eleven (11) item business process list shown in Topic 2 will not illustrated and discussed for Supporting Business Processes. Only four (4) items will be discussed:

- Process Purpose (List Item 2)
- Process Input (List Item 4)
- Process Flow (List Item 6)
- Process Output (List Item 7)

The specifics of each of these four items (and, indeed, the specifics of all eleven items) will differ by healthcare organization. There is no one description of each of these items which is suitable for every healthcare organization.

L1-T4. Healthcare Organization Human Resources Management Business Processes

All healthcare organizations (inpatient short-term, inpatient long-term, and outpatient) require qualified personnel to deliver health care safely, effectively, and efficiently. Human Resources Management Business Processes bear most of the responsibility for ensuring that the healthcare organization recruits and retains qualified personnel. These processes may not be the same for all healthcare organizations, but they do have some similarities. The people tasked with successful completion of these processes are Human Resources (HR) professionals.

The first organizational human resources department in the United States is generally considered to be the Personnel Department [bib#101] established in 1901 by the National Cash Register Company (now known as NCR [bib#102]). The oldest association for human resources professionals is considered to be the Chartered Institute of Personnel and Development (CIPD [bib#103]) established in 1913 in England as the Welfare Workers' Association (WWA). The Society for Human Resource Management (SHRM) [bib#104]:

> "*is the world's largest HR professional society, representing 300,000 members in more than 165 countries. For nearly seven decades, the Society has been the leading provider of resources serving the needs of HR professionals and advancing the practice of human resource management. SHRM has more than 575 affiliated chapters within the United States and subsidiary offices in China, India and United Arab Emirates*".

The American Society for Healthcare Human Resources Administration (ASHHRA) of the American Hospital Association (AHA): "*is the nation's only membership organization dedicated to meeting the needs of human resources professionals in health care*". ASHHRA offers a Certified in Healthcare Human Resources (CHHR) [bib#105] credential which defines the primary, but not the only, responsibilities of a healthcare human resources professional [bib#106] to be:

- "*Demonstrates knowledge of health care and healthcare human resource environments, provision of medical care, and healthcare workforce needs.*

- *Adapts healthcare-specific human resources knowledge to their individual healthcare organization's needs and goals.*

- *Provides strategic guidance in the interfacing of HR programs and practices to meet the overall mission and vision of the healthcare organization.*

- *Serves as a trusted advisor and partners with organization leadership on strategic initiatives, employee relations, and communication.*"

The personnel needs of healthcare organizations vary by the type of health care the organization delivers. Healthcare Human Resources professionals must ensure that organizational personnel are qualified to deliver that health care. This qualification to deliver health care is usually regulated at the state level.

> "*Most healthcare occupations are regulated by states, which means they require a license, certification, or registration. Licenses are typically issued by states to ensure that workers meet specific legal requirements to practice in an occupation. States have regulatory boards that set standards for the practice of a licensed occupation, but rules and eligibility may vary from state to state for the same occupation. Certifications may be required or optional to show skill competency.*
>
> *Certifications are usually offered by professional organizations, and some licenses are tied to the certification requirements ... Even if a state does not require a certification, employers may prefer that candidates be certified and a certification may therefore increase a candidate's chances of securing employment.*" (Website Source of Quote5 [bib#107])

The state licensing of healthcare professionals [bib#108] is generally recognized as having started in California and Texas in 1876. Alabama followed shortly thereafter in 1877. The United States Department of Labor, Bureau of Labor Statistics (BLS [bib#109]) produces the Occupational Outlook Handbook (OOH [bib#110]). The section on Healthcare Occupations [bib#111] lists 46 different healthcare occupations.

Healthcare Human Resources professionals must also be concerned with the safety of the healthcare personnel who work in the healthcare organization. They must be aware of safety regulations and guidelines such as those stipulated by the U.S. Department of Labor, Occupational Safety and Health Administration (OSHA) for healthcare workers [bib#112] and the Centers for Disease Control and Prevention (CDC), National Institute for Occupational Safety and Health (NIOSH) for healthcare workers [bib#113].

*****

> **Video** [bib#114]: *The video for Topic 4 –* **The Difference Between Respirators and Surgical Masks** *– is a YouTube video produced by U.S. Department of Labor. This video provides safety information for healthcare and other workers who require respiratory protection on the job. The link for the video is:* https://www.youtube.com/watch?v=ovSLAuY8ib8

*****

There are many different types of processes included in the Human Resources Management Business Processes and there are many ways to categorize these processes. In general, a common categorization is:

- New Employee Recruitment, Hiring, and Onboarding Processes
- Employee Compensation and Benefits Processes
- Employee Performance Evaluation and Incentives Processes
- Employee Training and Development Processes
- Employee End of Employment Processes
- Organizational Compliance with All Relevant Labor Law and Regulations

The specifics of Process Purpose, Process Input, Process Flow, and Process Output will differ for each of the six Human Resources Management Business Processes mentioned above. The specifics will differ by healthcare organization. There is no one description of each of these items which is suitable for every healthcare organization.

Process Purpose: In general, the purpose of all Human Resources Management Business Processes is to ensure that the healthcare organization has the personnel needed to efficiently and effectively deliver health care to the patient/customer.

Process Input: In general, Human Resources Management Business Processes begin with a formal request from the healthcare organization to fill a specific job.

Process Flow: The steps vary by the specific Human Resources Management Business Process. The steps for employee recruitment, for example, are different from those for payroll. The specifics will also vary by healthcare organization. However,

- Examples of a visualization for an employee payroll Process Flow can be found at the smartdraw, Payroll Swim Lane Flowchart [bib#115] website, the Creately, Payroll Workflow Chart [bib#116] website, and the Creately, HR Payroll Process Flow [bib#117] website.

- Examples of visualization for an employee onboarding Process Flow can be found at the Creately, Onboarding Flow Chart [bib#118] website and the Heflo Employee Onboarding [bib#119] website.

- Examples of visualization for an employee recruitment and hiring Process Flow can be found at the Creately, Human Resources [bib#120] website.

- An example of visualization for a human resources information system Process Flow can be found at the Creately, Human Resource Information System (Flowchart) [bib#121] website.

Process Output: In general, Human Resources Management Business Processes end when an employee ends employment with the healthcare organization.

There are many human resources information systems which target increasing the efficiency and effectiveness of Human Resources Management Business Processes. Many of the options are discussed at the Technology Advice (TA), TechnologyAdvice Human Resources Software Buyer's Guide [bib#122] website and the Capterra, Human Resource Software [bib#123] website. Some of these are free under certain conditions (e.g., for small companies). Examples include:

- Apptivo [bib#124]
- SimpleHRM [bib#125]
- HR.my [bib#126]

L1-T4. Healthcare Organization Financial Management Business Processes

All healthcare organizations (inpatient short-term, inpatient long-term, and outpatient) require adequate finances to deliver health care safely, effectively, and efficiently (e.g., revenue must match or exceed expenditures). Financial Management Business Processes bear most of the responsibility for tracking finances (expenditures and revenue) and ensuring that the finances of the healthcare organization are in good order (e.g., comply with all laws, regulations, and standard financial practices) - that the healthcare organization is financially sound and in good financial health. These processes may not be the same for all healthcare organizations, but they do have some similarities.

In larger healthcare organizations, the people tasked with successful completion of these processes are usually the organizational responsibility of the organization's Chief Financial Officer (CFO) [bib#127]. In smaller organizations, the CFO responsibilities may belong to someone with the title of Finance Director, Controller, or Accountant (for a small healthcare organization, the accountant may not be an employee of the organization, but rather an employee of an accounting firm). Some of the professional associations for those involved in organizational financial processes are:

- The American Finance Association (AFA) [bib#128]
- The Association for Finance Professionals (AFP) [bib#129]
- The Professional Accounting Society of America (PASA) [bib#130]
- The American Accounting Association (AAA) [bib#131]

The Healthcare Financial Management Association (HFMA [bib#132]) "*is the nation's premier membership organization for healthcare finance leaders ... Our mission is to lead the financial management of health care*". HFMA offers a Certified Healthcare Financial Professional (CHFP) [bib#133] credential.

There are many different types of processes included in the Financial Management Business Processes and there are many ways to categorize these processes. In general, a common categorization is:

- Collaborate to Develop Strategies to Meet the Organization's Short Term and Long Term Financial Goals

- Estimate the Amount of Capital the Organization Requires

- Implement a Capital Structure That Ensures the Sound Financial Operation of the Organization

- Implement and Monitor Financial Controls to Ensure the Financial Operations are Sound and Legal

The specifics of Process Purpose, Process Input, Process Flow, and Process Output will differ for each of the four Financial Management Business Processes mentioned above. The specifics will differ by healthcare organization. There is no one description of each of these items which is suitable for every healthcare organization.

Process Purpose: In general, the purpose of all Financial Management Business Processes is to ensure that the financial situation/health of the healthcare organization is sufficient for the healthcare organization to efficiently and effectively deliver health care to the patient/customer.

Process Input: In general, Financial Management Business Processes begin as soon as a healthcare organization needs money to efficiently and effectively deliver health care to the patient/customer.

Process Flow: The steps vary by the specific Financial Management Business Process. The specifics will also vary by healthcare organization. However,

- Examples of a visualization for an accounting Process Flow can be found at the Lucidchart, Accounting Flowchart [bib#134] website and Creately, Accounting Process Flow (Flowchart) [bib#135] website

- Examples of a visualization for financial reporting Process Flow can be found at the Creately, Financial Reporting Cycle (Flowchart) [bib#136] website

Process Output: In general, Financial Management Business Processes end when a healthcare organization no longer needs money to efficiently and effectively deliver health care to the patient/customer.

There are many financial management information systems which target increasing the efficiency and effectiveness of Financial Management Business Processes. Many of the options are discussed at the Financial Management Systems [bib#137] website (Company: Software Advice) and the Financial Management Software [bib#138] website (Company: Capterra). Some financial management and accounting software is free under certain conditions (e.g., for small companies). Examples include:

- GnuCash [bib#139]
- xTuple PostBooks [bib#140]
- ZipBooks [bib#141]
- Wave [bib#142]

Clearly, financial management is the management of money. The history of money [bib#143] is fascinating with some arguing that money was developed to replace barter and some arguing that it developed as a completely different system alongside barter. Historians believe that the first coins used as money [bib#144] for commerce were developed around 700 BC by the Lydians [bib#145] who lived in an area of what is now known as Turkey.

The United States dollar [bib#146] was created by Congress on April 2, 1792. The United States Treasury [bib#147] whose primary function has always been the "*management of the money resources of the United States*" was established on September 2, 1789. Alexander Hamilton [bib#148] took the oath of office as the first Secretary of the Treasury on September 11, 1789.

The production of paper money in the United States is the responsibility of the Treasury's Bureau of Engraving and Printing (BEP) [bib#149] which is also responsible for producing United States Postal Service stamps [bib#150]. The United States Mint [bib#151] produces United States legal tender currency coins. The United States Mint is an independent government agency [bib#152]. One facility of the United States Mint is Fort Knox [bib#153].

L1 Topic 5 (T5). What are healthcare organization management business processes?

Management Business Processes regulate and control the Operational Business Processes and the Supporting Business Processes. They do not usually have direct contact with customers. Examples of Management Business Processes in healthcare organizations – and in all organizations – are those related to governance, quality assurance, and strategic planning. Each healthcare organization has its own unique set of management business processes. However, there are some commonalities across all healthcare organizations:

Process Purpose: In general, it is to ensure that the healthcare organization's Operational Business Processes and Supporting Business Processes operate at the level of efficiency and effectiveness needed to deliver health care to the patient/customer.

Process Input: In general, the process is initiated when the healthcare organization is first formed – first becomes a legal entity.

Process Flow: The steps will vary greatly by type of healthcare organization and the specific management business process being implemented. This section addresses four common responsibilities of management business processes (listed below)

Process Output: In general, the process ends when the healthcare organization is dissolved – when it ceases to be a legal entity.

This section addresses:

- Functional versus Process-Oriented Management Business Processes
- Business Process Management Software

- Project Management Business Processes
- Strategic Plan Business Processes

L1-T5. Functional versus Process- Oriented Management Business Processes

Every organization is a composite of business processes. A key decision for those with responsibility for the implementation of Management Business Processes (responsibility for managing the organization) is whether to be a functional organization or a process-oriented organization. As a general rule one can say that a functional organization is one where specific functions/departments are the management focus and that a process-oriented organization is one where the customer view (use case parameters) is the management focus.

At some level, all organizations are structured by function (e.g., human resources, marketing, cardiology, pharmacy) and these are often referred to as departments. And the business processes of each department have a purpose of achieving a departmental goal which should lead to the achievement of an organizational objective or goal.

In a functional organization, department goals are set independent of the goals of other department. And they are often set without full consideration of how the department goal will affect the operation of other departments. In such a case, the processes in the various departments can get out of sync with each other.

For example, if a goal for the speed with which patients are treated and processed in the emergency room is set independently, then the number of patients ready to leave the emergency room may exceed the capacity of other departments to either discharge those patients or admit them to the hospital. The department goals of the emergency room, hospital discharge office, and hospital admitting office may be out-of-sync. As a result, the emergency room can become overcrowded with patients who no longer need treatment. There is no organizational way to leave the emergency room. The emergency room cannot accept new patients who need emergency room care.

In a process-oriented organization, department goals are set to support the efficient and effective operation of a specific process (a specific customer use case scenario). All departments involved in that use case have goals set in conjunction with each other. In such a case, the processes in the various departments are in sync with and related to each other.

For example, if the use case is the patient/customer perspective on an emergency room visit, then the goal for the speed with which patients are treated and processed in the emergency room is set in conjunction with goal the for the departments which discharge those patients or admit them to the hospital. The department goals of the emergency room, hospital discharge office, and hospital admitting office are in sync and related to each other. As a result, the patient/customer has an efficient emergency room experience and the organization has a smooth flow of patients through the emergency room.

Visualizations (diagrams) of the difference between these two approaches can be found at the Process and Functional Approaches in BPMN [bib#154] website.

The functional organizational approach encourages strong organizational silos. Organizational silos exist when members of departments have a primary loyalty and identification with their department and departmental co-workers rather than with the organization as a whole. Members of a silo do not like to share resources (e.g., information, supplies, ideas) with those outside the department.

In general, the process-oriented organization tries to manage silos using one of two basic strategies: 1) reduce or eliminate silos; or 2) connect and manage silos.

The first strategy (reduce or eliminate silos) generally agrees with the Business Dictionary [bib#155] which states that a Silo Mentality "*will reduce efficiency in the overall operation, reduce morale, and may contribute to the demise of a productive company culture*". The overall goal in this situation is to blur departmental boundaries and encourage people to identify with the healthcare organization as a whole (and a specific customer use case scenario) rather than with their department.

The second strategy (connect and manage silos) considers silos to be inevitable in an organization comprised of highly specialized and trained professionals. It is thought that silos must be networked and managed – but not eliminated – if the organization is to function well. The overall goal in this situation is to connect and network silos to build bigger and bigger silos. Departments, for example, are networked to build a division. Divisions are networked to build an organization. Each silo is encouraged to be a high functioning unit (team) networked to other units (teams); the organization is a team-of-teams - all oriented toward a larger organizational goal (specific customer use case scenarios)

There are many articles and reports on approaches to silos in healthcare organizations. Some of the resources on this topic are:

- Better Patient Flow Means Breaking Down the Silos [bib#156]
- Breaking Down Silos to Improve Patient Flow, Hospital Efficiency [bib#157]
- Quashing the Silos and Getting to Integrated Health Care [bib#158]
- Breaking Down Silos Is a Myth, Do This Instead [bib#159]
- The Need for a Team of Teams [bib#160]
- It Takes a Team of Teams to Transform Healthcare [bib#161]
- Fixing Healthcare Safety: Team of Teams [bib#162]

L1-T5. *Business Process Management Software*

The software tools briefly discussed for the Operational Business Processes and the Supporting Business Processes can be considered a form of business process management software, but there is a class of software tools specifically categorized as Business Process Management Suites/Software (BPMS). Such software suites are designed to do more than just automate some or all business processes; they are designed to help manage business processes. They are tools for Management Business Processes.

In fact, the first use of the term [bib#163] *Business Process Management (BPM)* is credited to Gartner [bib#164] which used the term to describe a class of software tools/suites – Business Process Management Suites

(BPMS) – it was evaluating in 2000. Gartner is also credited with first use of the term Enterprise Resource Planning (ERP) in 1990 as well as coining the term *Intelligent Business Process Management Suites (iBPMS)* to refer to Business Process Management Software/Suites (BPMS) which include support for analytics. Gartner iBPMS reviews can be found at its Reviews for Intelligent Business Process Management Suites (iBPMS [bib#165]) website. Reviewed software suites include:

- Whitestein Technologies, Living Systems Process Suite (LSPS) [bib#166]
- Creatio Studio [bib#167]
- BP Logix [bib#168]
- Genpact Cora [bib#169]
- Nintex [bib#170]

Some BPMS is available for free under certain conditions. Examples include:

- jSonic BPM [bib#171]
- Activiti [bib#172]

L1-T5. Project Management Business Processes

Sometimes a healthcare organization needs to accomplish something outside of the usual and routine business processes and this is usually done via a project. The Project Management Institute (PMI [bib#173]) is:

> "*the leading not-for-profit professional membership association for the project management profession ... Our professional resources and research deliver value for more than 2.9 million professionals working in nearly every country in the world*".

PMI offers a number of certificates [bib#174] including the Project Management Professional (PMP [bib#175]) certificate. PMI defines a project [bib#176] as:

"a temporary endeavor undertaken to create a unique product, service or result ...it is not a routine operation, but a specific set of operations designed to accomplish a singular goal ... The development of software for an improved business process, the construction of a building or bridge, the relief effort after a natural disaster, the expansion of sales into a new geographic market — all are projects."

Project management business processes involve: 1) Initiating; 2) Planning; 3) Executing; 4) Monitoring and Controlling; and 5) Closing.

Free templates and software are available for the Project Management Business Processes. Some of them are:

- Top Project Management Excel Templates [bib#177]
- Free Project Management Templates [bib#178]
- Asana Project Management Software [bib#179]
- Workfront Enterprise Project Management Software [bib#180]
- Zoho Project Management Software [bib#181]

Some Project Management Business Processes software is free under certain conditions. Examples include:

- OpenProject [bib#182]
- ProjectOpen [bib#183]
- LibrePlan [bib#184]
- ProjectLibre [bib#185]

An interesting article on this topic is *Business Process Management vs. Project Management: Differences You Need to Know* [bib#186].

L1-T5. Strategic Plan Business Processes

Another Management Business Process is strategic planning. The Business Dictionary defines strategic planning [bib#187] as a:

"systematic process of envisioning a desired future, and translating this vision into broadly defined goals or objectives and a sequence of steps to achieve them ... strategic planning begins with the desired-end and works backward to the current status .. strategic planning looks at the wider picture and is flexible in choice of its means."

Examples of a healthcare organization strategic plan are the:

- Mayo Clinic 2020 Initiative [bib#188]
- Massachusetts General Hospital ECOCH 2019-2021 Strategic Plan [bib#189]
- U.S. Department of Health and Human Services (HHS) Strategic Plan [bib#190]
- The American Dental Association (ADA) Strategic Plan [bib#191]
- American Academy of Hospice and Palliative Medicine Strategic Plan (AAPHM) Strategic Plan [bib#192]

There is no one template for a strategic planning document or universally agreed upon steps in a strategic planning process. As a general rule, however, a strategic plan and planning process includes the following six (6) steps:

1. Understanding and statement of the organization's mission, vision, and core businesses.

2. Understanding and statement of the organization's environment.

3. Understanding and statement of the organization's goals and objectives for the end of the strategic plan period (usually five years in the future).

4. Formulation and statement of a strategy to meet those goals and objectives in the organization's environment while adhering to the organization's mission, vision, and core businesses.

5. Implementation of the strategy (strategic plan)

6. Evaluation of the strategy during the strategic plan period to determine if the strategy/plan needs to be adjusted.

Step 2 is usually accomplished by using either an Environmental Scan or SWOT Analysis. The Business Dictionary defines Environmental Scanning [bib#193] as:

> "*Careful monitoring of an organization's internal and external environments for detecting early signs of opportunities and threats that may influence its current and future plans. In comparison, surveillance is confined to a specific objective or a narrow sector.*"

The Business Dictionary defines SWOT Analysis [bib#194] as:

> "*Situation analysis in which internal strengths and weaknesses of an organization, and external opportunities and threats faced by it are closely examined to chart a strategy. SWOT stands for strengths, weaknesses, opportunities, and threats.*"

*****

> *Video* [bib#195] : *The video for Topic 5 –* **Martin Reeves:** **Your Strategy Needs a Strategy** *– is a YouTube video produced by the TED Institute. This video discusses how to improve strategic planning. The link for the video is:* (https://www.youtube.com/watch?v=YE_ETgaFVo8

*****

Although there is no one template for a strategic planning document or universally agreed upon steps in a strategic planning process, templates and software are available. Some of them are:

- Free Strategic Planning Templates [bib#196]
- 14 Free SWOT Analysis Templates [bib#197]
- StrategyShare [bib#198]
- Cascade [bib#199]

- Smartdraw [bib#200]
- Envisio [bib#201]

Some useful additional resources on healthcare organization strategic planning are:

- Strategic Planning To Ensure Future Practice Success [bib#202]
- Why Strategic Planning is a Must for Practices [bib#203]
- Strategic Planning in Hospitals [bib#204]
- 5 Intangible Benefits Of Hospital Strategic Planning [bib#205]
- 6 Steps to Make Your Strategic Plan Really Strategic [bib#206]
- Your Strategic Plans Probably Aren't Strategic, or Even Plans [bib#207]
- All About Strategic Planning [bib#208]
- What Are The Basics Of Environmental Scanning as Part of the Strategic Planning Process? [bib#209]
- SWOT Analysis: What It Is and When to Use It [bib#210]

L1 Discussion Question: External/Environmental Challenges for Healthcare Organizations

One activity involved in the development of a strategic plan for any organization is trying to determine the challenges the organization might face from the environment; challenges from things external to the organization such as the availability of resources or mandatory requirements established by federal, state, or local governments.

What, in your opinion, are the biggest environmental challenges healthcare organizations will face in the next five to ten years?

L1 Quiz and "Create Your Own Healthcare Organization Business Processes"

L1 Quiz

<u>Question 1</u>

"A series of actions completed to achieve a specified organizational objective or goal" is a definition of a:

A. Business process
B. Business result
C. Process change
D. Health care outcome

The answer to this question is found in Topic 1 and in the Lesson One (L1) Quiz Answer Key at the end of the Lesson One (L1) Quiz.

<u>Question 2</u>

Which of the following is **NOT** generally considered to be a business process category?

A. Supporting business processes
B. Sunset business processes
C. Operational business processes
D. Management business processes

The answer to this question is found in Topic 1 and in the Lesson One (L1) Quiz Answer Key at the end of the Lesson One (L1) Quiz.

<u>Question 3</u>

If a business process is automated, a Use Case describes how the end user interacts with (views and uses) the business process software application.

A. True
B. False

The answer to this question is found in Topic 1 and in the Lesson One (L1) Quiz Answer Key at the end of the Lesson One (L1) Quiz.

Question 4

"A discipline involving any combination of modeling, automation, execution, control, measurement and optimization of business activity flows, in support of enterprise goals, spanning systems, employees, customers and partners within and beyond the enterprise boundaries." is a definition of:

A. Business Change Upgrades (BCU)
B. Physics
C. Business Process Management (BPM)
D. Business Physics Analogs (BPA)

The answer to this question is found in Topic 2 and in the Lesson One (L1) Quiz Answer Key at the end of the Lesson One (L1) Quiz.

Question 5

Healthcare organizations (all organizations) should not only document _____ processes, but also document the existence of all business processes; there should be a complete inventory of all business processes and their associated documents.

The answer to this question is found in Topic 2 and in the Lesson One (L1) Quiz Answer Key at the end of the Lesson One (L1) Quiz.

Question 6

The activity to transform the written business process document into a graphical visualization is called Business Process Mapping.

A. True
B. False

The answer to this question is found in Topic 2 and in the Lesson One (L1) Quiz Answer Key at the end of the Lesson One (L1) Quiz.

Question 7

Business processes which produce direct value for the customer (produce the organization's product and often have direct contact with the organization's customer) are usually called:

A. Operational Business Processes

B. Management Business Processes

C. Supporting Business Processes

The answer to this question is found in Topic 3 and in the Lesson One (L1) Quiz Answer Key at the end of the Lesson One (L1) Quiz.

Question 8

Which of the following is **NOT** usually considered a general operational business process category in a healthcare organization?

A. Personnel Hiring

B. Patient/Customer Discharge

C. Patient/Customer Intake

D. Health Care Delivery

The answer to this question is found in Topic 3 and in the Lesson One (L1) Quiz Answer Key at the end of the Lesson One (L1) Quiz.

Question 9

Health Care Delivery Business Processes are those which deliver health care. They are **EXACTLY** the same in all healthcare organizations.

A. True

B. False

The answer to this question is found in Topic 3 and in the Lesson One (L1) Quiz Answer Key at the end of the Lesson One (L1) Quiz.

Question 10

Business processes which support the Operational Business Processes as the "back office" functions which do not usually have direct contact with customers are usually called:

A. Supporting Business Processes

B. Exceptional Business Processes

C. Management Business Processes

The answer to this question is found in Topic 4 and in the Lesson One (L1) Quiz Answer Key at the end of the Lesson One (L1) Quiz.

Question 11

Which of the following is **NOT** usually considered a general supporting business process category in a healthcare organization?

A. Human Resources Management
B. Financial Management
C. Health Care Delivery

The answer to this question is found in Topic 4 and in the Lesson One (L1) Quiz Answer Key at the end of the Lesson One (L1) Quiz.

Question 12

Healthcare Human Resources professionals must ensure that organizational personnel are qualified to deliver the health care offered by that healthcare organization. The personnel needs of healthcare organizations are **EXACTLY** the same in all healthcare organizations.

A. True
B. False

The answer to this question is found in Topic 4 and in the Lesson One (L1) Quiz Answer Key at the end of the Lesson One (L1) Quiz.

Question 13

Business processes which regulate and control the Operational Business Processes and the Supporting Business Processes and do not usually have direct contact with customers are usually called:

A. Utilitarian Business Processes
B. Management Business Processes
C. Change-Oriented Business Processes

The answer to this question is found in Topic 5 and in the Lesson One (L1) Quiz Answer Key at the end of the Lesson One (L1) Quiz.

Question 14

As a general rule one can say that a functional organization is one where specific functions/departments are the _____ focus and that a process-oriented organization is one where the customer view (use case parameters) is the management focus.

The answer to this question is found in Topic 5 and in the Lesson One (L1) Quiz Answer Key at the end of the Lesson One (L1) Quiz.

Question 15

Organizational silos exist when members of departments have a primary loyalty and identification with their department and departmental co-workers rather than with the organization as a whole.

A. True
B. False

The answer to this question is found in Topic 5 and in the Lesson One (L1) Quiz Answer Key at the end of the Lesson One (L1) Quiz.

L1 Quiz Answer Key

Q1 = A; Q2 = B; Q3 = A; Q4 = C; Q5 = business; Q6 = A; Q7 = A; Q8 = A; Q9 = B; Q10 = A; Q11 = C; Q12 = B; Q13 = B; Q14 = management; Q15 = A

L1 "Create Your Own Healthcare Organization Business Processes"

In *Lesson Four*, you will *Design Healthcare Organization Business Processes*. This task requires that you synthesize content to create your own patient-centered business processes within a healthcare organization the way you would have things run in the best of all worlds. The type of healthcare organization is your choice (e.g., physical therapy office, dentist office, pharmacy, hospital, doctor's office).

It is suggested that your synthesized information be presented (formatted/designed) as a memo developed using word processing software (e.g., Microsoft Word). An example of a completed memo project is found in *Appendix B: Memo Example*. The memo is an artifact of the book which you can circulate to colleagues or use for a talk or presentation event. For the suggested memo project, you will need word processing software. There are many software options. Some are available at no cost such as Writer [bib#211] which is part of LibreOffice [bib#212].

Nine (9) content items and seven (7) format/design items are suggested for the electronic memo task to develop competency.   However, it is best not to wait until Lesson Four to begin to synthesize content to create your own business processes for a healthcare organization. The earlier in your learning path that you begin this creation process, the better your own business processes within a healthcare organization will be.

So in each lesson prior to Lesson Four, there will be an opportunity to begin to synthesize material – an opportunity to begin to create your own business processes within a healthcare organization using material presented in that lesson. Of the nine (9) suggested content items for the completed memo, six (6) are suggested for consideration in this lesson. Each one of the six is posted below and includes an expanded description as well as an example. They are:

Suggested Memo Content Item 1

   The name of your healthcare organization in which you will design your patient-centered business processes.

The name should be original and give some sense to healthcare consumers as to the healthcare products found in your organization.

Example: Charles Harbor General Hospital (CHGH)

Suggested Memo Content Item 2

A brief description of your healthcare organization; what your healthcare organization does.

The description should be a few sentences which concisely and clearly summarize for healthcare consumers the type of healthcare organization, its location, and its products.

Example: Charles Harbor General Hospital (CHGH) is a private, non-profit, general hospital in Massachusetts. It has an emergency room and a full range of clinical specialties (e.g., internal medicine, general surgery, oncology, cardiology, infectious disease, pediatrics).

Suggested Memo Content Item 3

A brief, broad overview of the most important Use Case for your patient-centered healthcare organization; that is, what are the most important requirements patients have for your healthcare organization?

The Use Case concept can be applied to a patient-centered healthcare organization's business processes regardless of whether the processes are automated. Such a Use Case describes how the patient/customer interacts with (views and uses) the healthcare organization's business processes. It describes the patient/customer requirements for doing business with the healthcare organization (what features does the patient/customer want). A Use Case provides a framework for the healthcare organization what the business processes are supposed to do (Use Case Business Process Management). There is no right or wrong answer to this question. It just has to be reasoned and make sense.

Example: CHGH patients want to feel confident in the health care they receive from CHGH; that, it patients want to have full confidence in the CHGH health care delivery personnel. Patients also want to feel respected and treated as individuals. Patients also want the facilities to be clean and comfortable.

Suggested Memo Content Item 4

A brief, broad overview of the Operational Business Processes most important to your Use Case.

Operational Business Processes (sometimes called Core Business Processes or Primary Business Processes) are the processes which produce direct value for the customer; they produce the organization's product and often have direct contact with the organization's customer. In a healthcare organization, these processes are those related to health care delivery. There is no right or wrong answer to this question. It just has to be reasoned and make sense.

Example: For the CHGH Use Case requirements to be met, CHGH must have superior, patient-centered health care delivery personnel and excellent health care delivery facilities and equipment.

Suggested Memo Content Item 5

A brief, broad overview of the Supporting Business Processes most important to your Use Case.

Supporting Business Processes (sometimes called Secondary Business Processes) support the Operational Business Processes. They are the "back office" functions which do not usually have direct contact with customers. Examples of Supporting Business Processes in healthcare organizations - and in all organizations - are those related to human resources, facilities, and financial management. There is no right or wrong answer to this question. It just has to be reasoned and make sense.

Example: For the CHGH Use Case requirements to be met, CHGH must have superior human resources personnel and processes to ensure that the health care delivery personnel are superior and patient-centered. CHGH also needs superior facilities personnel and processes to ensure that health care delivery facilities and equipment are superior, clean, and comfortable.

Suggested Memo Content Item 6

A brief description of how the Operational Business Processes and Supporting Business Processes are managed to ensure that they are functioning well and meeting the Use Case.

There is no right or wrong answer to this question. It just has to be reasoned and make sense.

Example: CHGH monitors the Operational Business Processes through patient surveys regarding whether they feel confident in the health care they receive from CHGH; that is, whether they have full confidence in the CHGH health care delivery personnel. Patients are also surveyed regarding whether they feel respected and treated as individuals as well as whether patients feel the facilities are clean and comfortable. If more than five percent of the survey respondents are dissatisfied with any of the items, then a review of the processes involved is undertaken. The review includes a review of human resources processes and facilities processes.

L1 Trivia Question and Virtual Field Trip

L1 Trivia Question

Almost everyone loves a trivia question – a question about a little known, but interesting, fun fact. Each lesson has one trivia question. The answer is in the Lesson One Trivia Question Answer section.

Question:

Information is a critical part of all business processes and business process management. George Washington valued information and envisioned an information infrastructure containing a "system of post roads and post offices" – a mail system. *He and many others at the time saw an "increasing need for a mail system to ensure" what?*

L1 Trivia Question Answer

The answer to the Lesson One trivia question is:

The free flow of information between citizens and their government.

For more information, please see:

- [Binding the Nation](#) [bib#213]
- [Postal Service Act](#) [bib#214]
- [United States Postal Service: An American History 1775 – 2006](#) [bib#215]

L1 Virtual Field Trip

Everyone loves a road trip/field trip so each lesson includes a "*virtual field trip*" to the often hidden places of interest on the web.

Lesson One's virtual field trip is to the [Smithsonian National Postal Museum](#) [bib#216]:

> "*The Museum's galleries explore America's postal history from colonial times to the present. Visitors learn how mail has been transported and the wondrous diversity of postage stamps.*"

The first [United States Postmaster General (PMG)](#) [bib#217] was Benjamin Franklin who was appointed by the Continental Congress in 1775. Benjamin Franklin had first been a Postmaster in 1737 when he was appointed Postmaster of Philadelphia when it was a British colony.

An important component of the [U.S. Postal Service](#) [bib#218] is the [United States Postal Inspection Service](#) [bib#219] whose mission is:

> "*to support and protect the U.S. Postal Service and its employees, infrastructure, and customers; enforce the laws that defend the nation's mail system from illegal or dangerous use; and ensure public trust in the mail*".

The [forerunner of this Service](#) [bib#220] was started by Benjamin Franklin in 1737. The first [Chief Postal Inspector](#) [bib#221] of the United States Postal Inspection System was [William Goddard](#) [bib#222] who was appointed in 1775 (the job title in 1775 was Surveyor of the Post).

*****

> *Video* [bib#223]: *The video for the Lesson One Virtual Field Trip –* ***We are the U.S. Postal Inspection Service*** *– is a YouTube video produced by the Smithsonian National Postal Museum. The video provides an overview of the activities of the members of the U.S. Postal Inspection Service. The link for the video is:*
> https://www.youtube.com/watch?v=Jrb2xb0ORXI

*****

Lesson Two (L2): Healthcare Organization Business Process Management Improvement and Innovation

Note: The above picture is adapted from the one by Mesh found on Unsplash
(https://unsplash.com/photos/9iY3Sqr1UWY)

L2 Competency Objective

This lesson provides an overview of healthcare organization business process management improvement and innovation. The competency objective is:

- Define healthcare organization business process management improvement and innovation

L2 Content and Discussion

This lesson provides an overview of healthcare organization business process management improvement and innovation. Upon successful completion of this lesson, you will be able to: define healthcare organization business process management improvement and innovation. There are topic questions, a discussion question, a quiz, a trivia question, and a field trip. The lesson should take 4 - 6 hours of work to successfully complete. There are also videos which provide supplemental content which can help you better define your personal learning path. There are many wonderful videos in the public domain which are relevant to the topics in this book.

This lesson addresses five (5) topics organized as questions. The questions/topics for Lesson Two are:

1. What is Business Process Improvement (BPI) in healthcare organizations?

2. How does the Business Process Re-engineering (BPR) improve healthcare organization business processes?

3. What are the research, development, and innovation business processes for healthcare organizations?

4. What are the technology transfer business processes for healthcare organizations?

5. What are the disruptive innovation and entrepreneurship business processes for healthcare organizations?

L2 Topic 1 (T1). What is Business Process Improvement (BPI) in healthcare organizations?

No healthcare organization – no organization – is perfect. All organizations need to continually pay attention to their business processes and ensure that they are functioning efficiently and effectively – and improve them as necessary. Such improvement is usually called Business Process

Improvement (BPI). A common strategy for BPI is use of the Business Process Management Lifecycle.

This section addresses:

- Overview of Business Process Management Lifecycle
- Five Phases of the Business Process Management Lifecycle

L2-T1. *Overview of Business Process Management Lifecycle*

As stated earlier, one component of good business process documentation is *Control Points and Measurements*. A control point is a place in the Business Process Flow where measurements are taken to ensure that the business process is functioning as intended. The measurement is evaluated against benchmarks set to determine when an organizational re-evaluation of the process is needed (e.g., a step which requires the review of qualified applicants for a job finds that the measurement for that step is 0 – no qualified applicants applied –- which serves as the benchmark to activate a review of why the number of applicants is 0 and discussion of what the organization can do to increase the number of qualified applicants).

If a measurement/value reaches a pre-specified value, then those responsible for business process management are activated to review the process for improvement/modification. The Business Process Improvement (BPI) strategy/review is activated. Sometimes this review looks at the one individual business process and sometimes it involves a review of that process and those business processes with which it interacts. This review, whether of one process or many processes, is often called the Business Process Management Lifecycle. The review may also be done routinely as well on one or more processes to ensure that the organization is operating as efficiently and effectively as possible.

*****

> **Video** [bib#224]: *The video for Topic 1 – **Business Process Management (BPM) Explained in Under 5 Minutes** – is a YouTube video produced by Medforce Technologies. The video provides an overview of Business Process Management (BPM). The link for the video is:*
> https://www.youtube.com/watch?v=iI6T3-7JxdU

*****

L2-T2. Five Phases of the Business Process Management Lifecycle

The Business Process Management Lifecycle is generally considered to have five (5) phases/components:

1. Design: Identify the process or processes to be reviewed and gather the existing information on the process(es). For example, gather the existing business process documentation and the control point measurements/values over some specified period of time. If any needed information is missing, gather that information. If more than one process is being reviewed, understand how those processes interact.

2. Modeling: Create a model of the process(es) which can be manipulated to determine the effect of changes in different variables and structures of importance in the process. This model can be created without automation, but an automated model using some of the software discussed in Lesson One is usually more effective and efficient for the purpose. Some find Automated Business Process Discovery (ABPD) software helpful in creating models. ABPD software [bib#225] records and examines the:

   > "*electronic footprints the users leave in the IT assets supporting the process … delivers the ability to take system data and automatically piece together 'as-is' business processes. It visually demonstrates process exceptions,*

unusual transactions, bottlenecks, deviations, weaknesses and potential risks in processes."

Examples of ABPD software are:

- Minit [bib#226]
- Worksoft [bib#227]

3. Execution: After modeling various scenarios, the optimal one - the modeled business process(es) structure most likely to achieve the organizational goal (e.g., to improve the control point measurements/values) is chosen. Once the optimal business process structure has been decided, it is executed/implemented in real time as the organization's business process replacing the one which was considered problematic.

4. Monitoring: The newly executed/implemented business process structure is monitored to see if it produces the outputs expected from the model. If it does not, then additional modeling occurs and a new optimal model chosen.

5. Optimization: Once the organization is satisfied that the optimal model has been chosen and is working, the implemented model is reviewed for optimization. It is reviewed to see if it needs to be slightly adjusted to ensure its functioning is optimized.

L2 Topic 2 (T2). How does the Business Process Re-engineering (BPR) improve healthcare organization business processes?

Sometimes the activity of the Business Process Management Lifecycle, which is sometimes called Business Process Improvement (BPI), indicates that more than an improvement to an existing business process or processes is needed. Sometimes the organization needs a massive change in the business processes to function efficiently and effectively. This change is usually called Business Process Re-engineering (BPR) although sometimes in is called Business Process Redesign.

This section addresses:

- Overview of Business Process Re-engineering (BPR)
- Business Process Re-engineering (BPR) Steps

L2-T2. Overview of Business Process Re-engineering (BPR)

The Business Dictionary defines Business Process Re-engineering (BPR [bib#228]) as the:

> "*Thorough rethinking of all business processes, job definitions, management systems, organizational structure, work flow, and underlying assumptions and beliefs. BPR's main objective is to break away from old ways of working, and effect radical (not incremental) redesign of processes to achieve dramatic improvements in critical areas (such as cost, quality, service, and response time) through the in-depth use of information technology.*"

One statement on the difference between [bib#229] Business Process Improvement (BPI) and Business Process Re-engineering (BPR) is:

> "*While BPI is an incremental setup that focuses on tinkering with the existing processes to improve them, BPR looks at the broader picture. BPI doesn't go against the grain; it identifies the process bottlenecks and recommends changes in specific functionalities. The process framework principally remains the same when BPI is into play. BPR, on the other hand, rejects the existing rules and often takes an unconventional route to redo processes from a high-level management perspective.*
>
> *Another good analogy can be seen in trying to live a healthy lifestyle. BPI might involve finding a way to get to the gym more often and eat less sugar. But BPR is an entire lifestyle change that starts with how you buy food, how you incorporate movement and exercise into your day, and how to reduce stress.*"

The concept of Business Process Re-engineering (BPR) is generally considered to have been introduced by Michael M. Hammer [bib#230] in his 1990 Harvard Business Review article entitled *Reengineering Work: Don't Automate, Obliterate* [bib#231]. One of his main points in the article is that automating bad business processes only makes them work badly much more quickly. Therefore, bad business processes should not be automated, but obliterated through re-engineering of those processes. He states that:

> "*Reengineering triggers changes of many kinds, not just of the business process itself. Job designs, organizational structures, management systems—anything associated with the process—must be refashioned in an integrated way. In other words, reengineering is a tremendous effort that mandates change in many areas of the organization.*"

*****

> *Video* [bib#232]: *The video for Topic 2 –* **What's the Big Deal with Business Process Reengineering?** *– is a YouTube video produced by the Panorama Consulting Group. The video provides an overview of the importance of re-engineering business processes. The link for the video is:*
> https://www.youtube.com/watch?v=ee8iGNfem50

*****

L2-T2. Business Process Re-engineering (BPR) Steps

Thus, the Business Process Re-engineering (BPR) steps are goal-oriented (outcome-oriented) steps. There is no agreement on the specific steps involved in BPR, but in general the steps are:

Step 1: Define the goals (outcomes, end results) of the business process(es) re-engineering. State what the organization intends to achieve with this particular BPR and why achievement is important for the organization. These goals (outcomes, end results) should reflect the customer's (patient's) point-of-view. The BPR should improve organizational function and value for the customers/patients.

Step 2: Identify and analyze the existing process(es) involved in the BPR. Before starting any BPR, the process(es) to be re-engineered must be identified. The process(es) must also be analyzed and fully understood regarding the each process' role within organizational functioning, how it operates (e.g., which personnel are involved), and its current performance. The current effect of each process on value for the customer/patient must be understood.

Step 3: Develop and test various models of a new business process or processes. Once the existing process or processes involved in the BPR are understood, identify changes that should be made to achieve the goal (outcome, end result) identified in Step 1. Create models reflecting those indicated changes. Test the models and choose the optimal one for implementation.

Step 4: Implement the re-engineered process(es). Replace the existing process(es) identified in Step 2 with the optimal model identified in Step 3. Monitor and evaluate the implemented process(es) with respect to function efficiency and effect on the goals stated in Step 1. Optimize the process functioning as needed.

Some additional helpful information on BPR can be found in the following articles:

- Business Process Re-engineering Application in Healthcare in a Relation to Health Information Systems [bib#233]

- Making Your Business More Competitive with Business Process Reengineering (BPR) [bib#234]

- Business Process Reengineering in Healthcare: Literature Review on the Methodologies and Approaches [bib#235]

L2 Topic 3 (T3). What are the research, development, and innovation business processes for healthcare organizations?

Sometimes Business Process Improvement (BPI) and Business Process Re-engineering (BPR) are not sufficient for competitive organizational functioning. The organization needs something else – something new – something innovative. Some organizations have business processes dedicated to generating research, development, and/or innovation either for their own use or for sale to others. Other organizations do not, but do have business processes dedicated to staying aware of innovations of relevance, determining which to use, and implementing them. Still other organizations have neither.

This section addresses:

- Difference Between Research, Development, and Innovation
- Types of Innovation
- Business Processes for Innovation

L2-T3. Difference Between Research, Development, and Innovation

There is often some confusion about the difference between business processes dedicated to research versus development versus innovation. They are different.

Business Dictionary defines research [bib#236] as the:

> "*Systematic investigative process employed to increase or revise current knowledge by discovering new facts. It is divided into two general categories: (1) Basic research is inquiry aimed at increasing scientific knowledge, and (2) Applied research is effort aimed at using basic research for solving problems or developing new processes, products, or techniques.*"

Business Dictionary defines development [bib#237] as:

"1. The systematic use of scientific and technical knowledge to meet specific objectives or requirements. 2. An extension of the theoretical or practical aspects of a concept, design, discovery, or invention."

Business Dictionary defines innovation [bib#238] as:

"*The process of translating an idea or invention into a good or service that creates value or for which customers will pay. To be called an innovation, an idea must be replicable at an economical cost and must satisfy a specific need.*"

As can be seen in the definition of innovation, another important term in the discussion of research, development, and innovation is the term *invention*. Business Dictionary defines invention [bib#239] as a:

"*New scientific or technical idea, and the means of its embodiment or accomplishment. To be patentable, an invention must be novel, have utility, and be non-obvious. To be called an invention, an idea only needs to be proven as workable. But to be called an innovation, it must also be replicable at an economical cost, and must satisfy a specific need. That's why only a few inventions lead to innovations because not all of them are economically feasible.*"

Thus the difference and relationship between the terms research, development, invention and innovation is: research can lead to development which can lead to an invention with can lead to innovation (research > development > invention > innovation).

One health care delivery example of this difference and relationship is penicillin where research on bacteria led to the development of antibacterials (specifically, penicillin) which led to the invention of a form of penicillin which could be used for drug trials on mice and humans which led to the innovation of large scale production of antibiotics (especially penicillin) and their routine use in health care delivery.

Alexander Fleming [bib#240] is generally credited with the discovery of penicillin in 1928 (research). Fleming's source of penicillin – fermentation of

Penicillin mold – was scaled up to production levels (innovation) in the United States during World War II primarily to treat injured soldiers. Much of the credit for this increased production capacity is given to Abbott Laboratories [bib#241] and the United States Department of Agriculture, Northern Regional Research Laboratory (NRRL) in Illinois. NRRL is now called the National Center for Agricultural Utilization Research (NCAUR [bib#242]).

So effective was the ability to scale that the production of penicillin in the United States went from 21 billion units in 1943 to 8.8 trillion units in 1945. On March 15, 1945 penicillin became available for civilian use in the United States (no longer restricted to military use).

*****

Video [bib#243]: *The video for Topic 3 –* **First Use of Penicillin** *– is a YouTube video produced by Yale University. The video describes one of the first non-military uses of penicillin which saved a woman's life who had developed an infection after giving birth. The link for the video is:* https://www.youtube.com/watch?v=rnrnLf9DjpA

*****

Penicillin innovation took another step forward when John C. Sheehan [bib#244] – a synthetic organic chemist – completed the first total synthesis of penicillin in 1957. Until this synthetic form existed, all penicillin had to be produced via fermentation of mold. Sheehan's synthesis also produced the capability to produce customized forms of penicillin targeting specific bacteria.

Although Sheehan's work was directed and methodical with the goal of total synthesis of penicillin, Fleming's penicillin work is generally considered to be accidental Fleming is generally considered to have accidentally discovered penicillin. But Fleming is not alone in his accidental contributions. In general the following are also considered accidental inventions/innovations:

- Microwave Oven – Percy L. Spencer [bib#245]
- Teflon – Roy Plunkett [bib#246]

- Bakelite – Leo Baekeland [bib#247]
- X-Rays – Wilhelm Roentgen [bib#248]
- Super Glue – Harry Coover [bib#249]
- Saccharin – Ira Remsen [bib#250] and Constantin Fahlberg [bib#251]
- Pacemaker – Wilson Greatbatch [bib#252]

Given the accidental nature of some of the most interesting inventions/innovations in history, a paraphrase of the famous line from the movie Ratatouille [bib#253] might be appropriate… Not everyone can be an inventor/innovator; but the best invention/innovation can come from anyone and anywhere.

Additional interesting resources on the topic are:

- Penicillin's Discovery and Antibiotic Resistance: Lessons for the Future? [bib#254]
- The Real Story Behind Penicillin [bib#255]
- A Brief History of the Antibiotic Era: Lessons Learned and Challenges for the Future [bib#256]
- The Enchanted Ring: The Untold Story of Penicillin [bib#257]

L2-T3. Types of Innovation

In general, innovation is considered to be in one of three categories [bib#258]:

- Product/Technology Innovation – bringing a new product/technology or an existing product with new technology to market (produced at scale at a reasonable cost which meets a consumer need). Examples include the initial introduction of the Apple computer and cars with air conditioning. In health care delivery, an example might include introduction of a new prescription drug available to consumers.

- Process Innovation – a new method/process for producing products at scale and at a reasonable cost. The classic example is Henry Ford's introduction of the moving assembly line to produce cars. In health care delivery, an example might be the introduction of the triage system [bib#259] in 1792 by Dominique Jean Larrey [bib#260] to organize and treat battlefield casualties.

- Business Model Innovation - a new method (a new business model) for selling a product to consumers. Examples include rideshare services such as Uber and Lyft which are a new business model for the individual-pay-for-a-ride service (traditional business model = taxi) as well as AirBnB which can be considered to be a new business model for lodging services (traditional business model = hotel). An example in health care delivery might be Health Maintenance Organizations (HMOs).

Some additional items considered major healthcare innovations are the hard hat, car airbag, fly swatter, sidewalk, and the window screen which are listed in 100 Objects That Shaped Public Health [bib#261]. Items listed in 20 Years of Healthcare Advances [bib#262] include the use of statins for secondary prevention in cardiology, genomics, and patient reported outcomes measures in orthopedics.

L2-T3. Business Processes for Innovation

Most organizations seek to be innovative or at least stay up-to-date and current (to adopt as soon as possible the relevant innovations developed elsewhere). Some suggest that those organizations which truly seek to be innovative must have business processes which encourage and support innovation. Those business processes must include innovation-friendly management processes which support an organizational structure [bib#263] in which:

- All employees think like innovators
- All employees have a precise, shared definition of innovation
- There are comprehensive organization-wide innovation metrics
- There are accountable and capable organizational innovation leaders
- There are innovation-friendly management processes

Those organizations which wish to adopt innovations as soon as possible (be up-to-date and current) must devote some business processes to staying aware of relevant innovations and determining how to implement them. Such business processes may be dedicated to ensuring that employees:

- Stay aware of what the competition is doing regarding innovation
- Attend relevant innovation conferences and meetings
- Network with other relevant professionals interested in innovation
- Read the current literature on relevant innovation

For health care delivery innovations, such literature may include that available from Cochrane [bib#264]. The motto of Cochrane is: "Trusted evidence. Informed decisions. Better health." The primary Cochrane evidence methodology is the systematic review [bib#265]. These systematic reviews are published in the Cochrane Library [bib#266] and discuss possible innovations in health care delivery. Each systematic review:

> "*summarises the results of available carefully designed healthcare studies (controlled trials) and provides a high level of evidence on the effectiveness of healthcare interventions. Judgments may be made about the evidence and inform recommendations for healthcare.*"

Additional interesting resources on the topic are:

- International Association of Innovation Professionals (IAOIP) [bib#267]
- Successful Innovation through Business Process Management [bib#268]
- What Has Innovation to Do with Business Process Management? [bib#269]
- Innovation as a Business Process [bib#270]

L2 Topic 4 (T4). What are the technology transfer business processes for healthcare organizations?

The business processes which move a concept/discovery from research to development to invention to innovation are often called technology transfer processes. This section addresses these and associated business processes and concepts.

Specifically, this section addresses:

- Technology Transfer, Innovation Diffusion, and Product Adoption
- Healthcare Research and Development (R&D)
- Healthcare Innovation Centers

L2-T4. Technology Transfer, Innovation Diffusion, and Product Adoption

Sometimes there is confusion between the terms technology transfer, innovation diffusion, and product adopters. They are related, but not the same. Technology transfer concerns the process of developing an innovation; innovation diffusion concerns how use of that innovation spreads through a society; and product adoption defines how an individual consumer chooses to use an innovative product.

- Business Dictionary defines technology transfer [bib#271] as:

    "1. Assignment of technological intellectual property, developed and generated in one place, to another through legal means such as technology licensing or franchising. 2. Process of converting scientific and technological advances into marketable goods or services."

- Business Dictionary defines innovation diffusion [bib#272] as the:

"Theory that every market has groups of customers who differ in their readiness and willingness to adopt a new product. And, that an innovative product spreads (diffuses) through a market not in one straight course but in successive, overlapping waves.

Most populations show the following pattern in the adoption of new consumer goods: innovators (2 percent of population), early adopters (14 percent), early majority (34 percent), late majority (34 percent), and laggards (16 percent)."

- Business Dictionary defines product adoption [bib#273] as the:

  "Five-stage mental process all prospective customers go through from learning of a new product to becoming loyal customers or rejecting it. These stages are (1) Awareness: prospects come to know about a product but lack sufficient information about it; (2) Interest: they try to get more information; (3) Evaluation: they consider whether the product is beneficial;

  (4) Trial: they make the first purchase to determine its worth or usefulness; (5) Adoption/Rejection: they decide to adopt it, or look for something else. Another explanation is that the customer moves from a cognitive state (being aware and informed) to the emotional state (liking and preference) and finally to the behavioral or cognitive state (deciding and purchasing)."

Those organizations which have business processes dedicated to generating research, development, and/or innovation either for their own use or for sale to others usually have technology transfer processes in place.

Other organizations which try to stay current or up-to-date on innovations may have business processes which enable them to be innovators or early adopters in innovation diffusion. Such business processes may reflect the stages in the product adoption:

1. Business processes which enable the organization to be aware of the existence of an innovative product early even if sufficient information to make a decision about its use is lacking

2. Business processes which gather more information about the innovative product

3. Business processes which evaluate whether use of the innovative product is an improvement for the organization

4. Business processes which demo the innovative product to gather additional information on whether purchase of the product is indicated for the organization

5. Business processes which decide whether to purchase and use the innovative product (product adoption) or not (product rejection)

The first formal studies of the innovation diffusion (diffusion of innovations) is generally credited to the work of Gabriel Tarde [bib#274] in sociology on the "*laws of imitation*" published in 1890. However, Everett Rogers [bib#275] is credited with developing the first theory of innovation diffusion (diffusion of innovation) which was published in his book entitled *Diffusion of Innovations* [bib#276] which was first published in 1962.

Many of the organizations with internal technology transfer processes in place have official technology transfer offices or departments. Those departments within universities have an association – The Association of University Technology Managers (AUTM [bib#277]) which is a:

"*leader in efforts to educate, promote and inspire professionals to support the development of academic research that changes the world and drives innovation forward ... Our members work closely with commercial partners to transform ideas into opportunities, resulting in the creation each year of thousands of products, services and start-ups, and millions of dollars in economic development."*

Universities have always devoted business processes to scholarship and research, but their ability to engage in innovation was not straightforward until the passage of *The University and Small Business Patent Procedures Act of 1980* (commonly referred to as "*Bayh-Dole*" [bib#278]). Prior to Bayh-Dole, discoveries/inventions made using federal money in universities (or small businesses or non-profits) belonged to the federal government; any patents associated with such discoveries were granted to the federal government. The federal government, however, was not and is not particularly effective in moving the research/discovery to the innovation phase; the federal government is not particularly effective in technology transfer.

Bayh-Dole allows the patents (and royalties from those patents) to belong to the organization (university, small business, non-profit) making the discovery/invention. This change allowed technology transfer to happen via the universities, small businesses, and non-profits who proved to be better than the federal government at developing partnerships to commercialize discoveries/inventions (innovation) made with federal money.

The granting of patents and the registration of trademarks is the responsibility of the United States Patent and Trademark Office (USPTO [bib#279]) which was established in 1802 [bib#280]. Patents, trademarks, and copyrights protect intellectual property [bib#281] which are creations of human thought and intellect. Intellectual property is, in fact considered so important in the United States that it is protected under Article I, Section 8, Clause 8 [bib#282] of the United States Constitution. The clause states [bib#283]:

[The Congress shall have power] "To promote the progress of science and useful arts, by securing for limited times to authors and inventors the exclusive right to their respective writings and discoveries."

Additional interesting resources on the topic are:

- Technology Transfer: From the Research Bench to Commercialization: Part 1: Intellectual Property Rights—Basics of Patents and Copyrights [bib#284]
- Technology Transfer: From the Research Bench to Commercialization: Part 2: The Commercialization Process [bib#285]
- Bayh-Dole Regulations [bib#286]
- Bayh-Dole Act: Everything You Need to Know [bib#287]
- The Importance of the Bayh-Dole Act [bib#288]
- The Patent Office Pony, A History of the Early Patent Office [bib#289]

L2-T4. Healthcare Research and Development (R&D)

Some healthcare research and development occurs in universities. Other organizations – including healthcare organizations – also devote business processes to research and development. Some of the research and development is funded by the organizations themselves and some is funded by organizations external to the healthcare organization. According to a report by Research America [bib#290] entitled *U.S. Investments in Medical and Health Research and Development* [bib#291], a total of $171.8 billion was spent in the United States on medical and health Research and Development in 2016. Of this:

- $115.9 billion was spent by industry (e.g., pharmaceutical companies)
- $37.6 billion was spent by federal agencies (e.g., National Institutes of Health)
- $12.5 billion was spent by universities (and other academic and research institutions), independent research institutions (IRI), and independent hospitals
- $2.7 billion was spent by foundations
- $1.7 billion was spent by state and local governments
- $1.4 billion was spent by voluntary associations and professional societies

*****

Video [bib#292]: *The video for Topic 4 –* **NIH: National Institutes of Health** *– is a YouTube video produced by the Montgomery County Chamber of Commerce (MCCC). The video provides an overview of the past, present and future of the NIH. The link for the video is:*
https://www.youtube.com/watch?v=ezpi8J1UQA0

*****

Northwestern University is generally recognized as the academic institution with the most patent/licensing income primarily because of Lyrica [bib#293] which has generated more than one billion dollars [bib#294] in revenue for the university from the patent license. Lyrica is the brand name for pregabalin [bib#295] which was synthesized in 1990 by Richard Bruce Silverman [bib#296], a chemist as Northwestern University. Because of Bayh-Dole, Northwestern was able to enter into a partnership with Parke-Davis [bib#297], then a part of Warner-Lambert [bib#298], who brought pregabalin to market as Lyrica. Parke-Davis and Warner-Lambert are now part of Pfizer [bib#299].

The Pfizer company [bib#300] is the largest pharmaceutical company by annual revenue (approximately $50 billion); Pfizer spends approximately $8 billion per year on research and development.

The largest medical device company is Medtronic [bib#301] with approximately $30 billion in annual revenue; Medtronic spends approximately $1.5 billion per year on research and development.

The largest healthcare products company is McKesson [bib#302] with approximately $250 million in annual revenue; McKesson currently spends approximately $125 million per year on research and development.

L2-T4. Healthcare Innovation Centers

Innovation centers can play an important role in technology transfer business processes. Most are part of a larger organization. Almost all innovation centers provide advice on ways organizational discoveries/inventions can progress to the innovation state. Some provide funding to speed that progress.

Examples of innovation centers based in universities are:

- Geisinger, Center for Pharmacy Innovation and Outcomes (CPIO) [bib#303] whose:

    "*mission is to conduct, implement, and disseminate research to optimize medication use by leveraging a highly evolved health IT infrastructure, applying robust data including patient-reported information and a growing genomic reservoir, and deploying trained and highly skilled clinical pharmacists.*"

- Northwestern University, Center for Primary Care Innovation [bib#304] which:

    "*works to develop novel methods that will transform primary care. Our goals are to attract talented Northwestern trainees to primary care, test innovative ways to improve care delivery and to promote the adoption of innovative best practices.*"

- Thomas Jefferson University Innovation [bib#305] and Accelerator Zone [bib#306] to create an "*entrepreneurial ecosystem to advance the commercialization of new technologies*" with the Accelerator Zone serving as "*a platform to engage and unleash creative, entrepreneurial talent*".

- University of Maryland, Center for Innovative Pharmacy Solutions (CIPS) [bib#307]:

> "*is a national resource center and leader in the development of innovative patient care and business solutions to health problems ... CIPS captures the intellectual contributions and skills of pharmacists as they create pharmacist-directed patient care models that improve clinical outcomes, ensure medication adherence, and reduce health care costs.*"

- University of North Carolina (UNC), Center for Health Innovation [bib#308] which focuses on the:

> "*development of patient-centered innovations designed to address the current challenges facing our nation's health care delivery system related to cost efficiency, quality of care, innovative health care delivery, and alignment of incentives among industry participants.*"

- University of Pennsylvania, Center for Health Care Innovation [bib#309] which:

> "*facilitates the rapid, disciplined development, testing and implementation of new strategies to reimagine health care delivery for dramatically better value, patient outcomes, and experience. ... We believe the best way to make significant improvements to patient health and care delivery is to experiment quickly at low cost - scaling only once we find high impact solutions.*"

- University of South Carolina, Kennedy Pharmacy Innovation Center [bib#310] which:

> "*creates and fuels an influential cadre of pharmacists and educators equipped with a vibrant, innovative, and entrepreneurial spirit to conquer the challenges of the changing healthcare landscape and transform the practice of pharmacy*".

- Center for Research and Education in Technology (CRET), Innovation Centers (IC) [bib#311]:

  > "*are designed like a private sector dental office. The agreement is that the dental school builds the IC and funds the staff. In return, CRET provides all the equipment and merchandise for the IC for free. There are six different operatories; fully furnished by six different manufacturers. Dental Students have the opportunity to learn and use the latest technology and provide feedback to the manufacturers via evaluation surveys.*"

Innovation centers can also be found in hospitals. Some of them can be found in 58 hospitals with innovation programs: 2017 [bib#312]. Some of those listed are:

- Cleveland Clinic, Innovations [bib#313] which is the "*commercialization arm of Cleveland Clinic, turns medical breakthrough inventions of our caregivers into patient-benefiting medical products and companies.*"

- Massachusetts General Hospital (MGH), Innovation Programs [bib#314] which are "*developing creative new ways to improve the delivery of healthcare, reduce disparities and lower the cost of care*".

- Mayo Clinic, Center for Innovation (CFI) [bib#315] which starts "*with big ideas around people's needs, frame them as opportunities, define and refine the concept and move fast to validate tangible models that can be scaled*".

A recent survey by Beckers [bib#316] asked healthcare executives "*What healthcare system comes to mind as a model for innovation?*" The top five responses were:

- Mayo Clinic [bib#317]
- Kaiser Permanente [bib#318]

- Cleveland Clinic [bib#319]
- Geisinger Health System [bib#320]
- Intermountain Healthcare [bib#321]

A few other interesting innovation centers are:

- The collaboration between [bib#322] the American Dental Association (ADA) and MATTER [bib#323] (a health care innovation incubator) to "*work together to accelerate the development of new technologies that improve oral health*".

- National Community Pharmacists Association (NCPA), Innovation Center [bib#324]:

  "*whose mission is to further assist and accelerate the evolution of independent community pharmacies in the changing health care environment ... develops and executes programs that inform and educate community pharmacists, allowing them to realize the opportunities in an evolving health care market. In addition, it demonstrates, researches, and supports new and expanded roles for community pharmacists.*"

- Agency for Healthcare Research and Quality (AHRQ), Healthcare Innovations Exchange [bib#325]:

  "*whose purpose is "to speed the implementation of new and better ways of delivering health care ... offers busy health professionals and researchers the opportunity to share, learn about, and ultimately adopt evidence-based innovations and tools suitable for a range of health care settings and populations ...*

  defines an innovation as the implementation of new or altered products, services, processes, systems, policies, organizational structures, or business models that aim to improve one or more domains of health care quality or reduce health care disparities."

Many of the innovation centers sponsor contests or give awards to spur innovation within their organizations and/or the community at large. Two websites which provide innovation challenges, contests, and awards in health and other areas for the public-at-large are:

- Challenge.gov [bib#326] where "*members of the public compete to help the U.S. government solve problems big and small. Browse through challenges and submit your ideas for a chance to win*". Challenges are sponsored by federal agencies including challenges from the Department of Health and Human Services (HHS).

- Innocentive [bib#327] which is "*the global pioneer in crowdsourced innovation. We leverage the power of the crowd to help organizations of all sizes solve their critical business, scientific, and technical problems*". The specific challenges, many related to health, are listed in the Challenge Center.

L2 Topic 5 (T5). What are the disruptive innovation and entrepreneurship business processes for healthcare organizations?

Some innovations are small and some are a breakthrough. Some innovations are so different from what has come before and what exists that they are called disruptive innovations. Such disruptive innovations have their own unique business processes which are often associated with entrepreneurship.

Specifically, this section addresses:

- Disruptive Innovation
- Entrepreneurship
- Business Plan

L2-T5. *Disruptive Innovation*

Disruptive innovations are innovations which – over time - tend to make existing technologies/organizations obsolete. For that reason, disruptive innovations usually originate outside of existing organizations – in smaller organizations which grow and replace larger organizations. One example of a disruptive innovation is the telephone (and telephone companies) which replaced the telegraph (and telegraph companies).

The term and the theory of disruptive innovation is credited to Clayton M. Christiansen [bib#328] which he introduced and developed in many published works including his:

- 1995 article: *Disruptive Technologies: Catching the Wave [bib#329]*

- 1997 book: *Innovator's Dilemma: When New Technologies Cause Great Firms to Fail* [bib#330]

- 2013 book: *Innovators Solution: The Innovator's Solution: Creating and Sustaining Successful Growth* [bib#331]

Christiansen defines disruptive innovations [bib#332] as:

"a process whereby a smaller company with fewer resources is able to successfully challenge established incumbent businesses. Specifically, as incumbents focus on improving their products and services for their most demanding (and usually most profitable) customers, they exceed the needs of some segments and ignore the needs of others.

Entrants that prove disruptive begin by successfully targeting those overlooked segments, gaining a foothold by delivering more-suitable functionality frequently at a lower price. Incumbents, chasing higher profitability in more-demanding segments, tend not to respond vigorously. Entrants then move upmarket, delivering the performance that incumbents' mainstream customers require, while preserving the advantages that drove their early success. When mainstream customers start adopting the entrants' offerings in volume, disruption has occurred."

Christiansen has stated that disruptive innovations are necessary in the health care industry, but more difficult to accomplish than in other industries. Disruptions are particularly necessary in the healthcare business models, treatments for chronic diseases, and the healthcare reimbursement system. He discusses this situation in some detail in his 2009 book entitled *The Innovator's Prescription: A Disruptive Solution for Health Care* [bib#333] (co-authored with Jerome H. Grossman M.D. and Jason Hwang M.D. A multi-page summary of the book can be found at the SOUNDVIEW Executive Book Summaries [bib#334]

*****

Video [bib#335]: *The video for Topic 5 – **The Innovator's Prescription: A Disruptive Solution to Health Care** – is a YouTube video produced by the Colorado Medical Society. The video is of a talk given by Jason Hwang to the Society about the book he co-authored entitled "The Innovator's Prescription: A Disruptive Solution to Health Care". The link for the video is:*
https://www.youtube.com/watch?v=9DUKAGumqWw

*****

Additional interesting resources on the topic are:

- Christiansen Institute Topics: Healthcare [bib#336], especially How Disruption Can Finally Revolutionize Healthcare [bib#337]
- Will Disruptive Innovations Cure Health Care? [bib#338]
- Harnessing Disruptive Innovation in Health Care [bib#339]
- Disruptive Innovation In Health Care Delivery: A Framework For Business-Model Innovation [bib#340]
- Is health care ready for disruptive innovation? (part one) [bib#341]
- Is health care ready for disruptive innovation? (part two) [bib#342]

- [Is health care ready for disruptive innovation? (part three)](#) [bib#343]
- [New Marketplace Survey: The Sources of Health Care Innovation](#) [bib#344]
- [5 Ways to Drive Disruptive Innovation in Healthcare](#) [bib#345]

L2-T5. Entrepreneurship

The most common location for a disruptive innovation to originate is in a new organization (a start-up), not an existing organization. Existing organizations which discover/invent a potential innovation will either commercialize it within their existing organization or create a new one (a spin-off) to commercialize that potential innovation.

Sometimes organizations will spin-off a section of the organization, not for innovation, but to increase the efficiency and effectiveness of existing business processes. One of the best known examples of the latter case in healthcare is the Community Health Systems (CHS [bib#346]) spin-off of a portion of the organization [bib#347] into Quorum Health Corporation (QHC [bib#348]) in 2016.

The creation of a start-up or a spin-off for innovation purposes is generally considered entrepreneurship which the Business Dictionary defines as [bib#349] the:

> "capacity and willingness to develop, organize and manage a business venture along with any of its risks in order to make a profit. The most obvious example of entrepreneurship is the starting of new businesses ... Entrepreneurial spirit is characterized by innovation and risk-taking, and is an essential part of a nation's ability to succeed in an ever changing and increasingly competitive global marketplace."

Some of the entrepreneurial spin-offs were started by universities. Some of those related to health and healthcare are:

- Antheia [bib#350] which develops "*next generation plant-inspired medicines*"; Stanford University [bib#351]

- Sapience Therapeutics [bib#352] "*is focused on discovering and developing peptide-based therapeutics to previously 'undruggable' targets for major unmet medical needs, particularly high mortality cancers*"; Columbia University [bib#353]

- Synlogic [bib#354] which brings "*innovative living medicines to patients by using the tools and principles of synthetic biology to genetically re-program beneficial bacteria*"; Massachusetts Institute of Technology (MIT) [bib#355]

The spin-off companies from one university, Scripps Research – formerly The Scripps Research Institute (TSRI) – are almost all health and health care related. Scripps Research has more than 80 spin-off companies [bib#356] since 1980. Company creation/entrepreneurship is coordinated through its Office of Technology Development (OTD [bib#357]).

Hospitals and health systems have also started some entrepreneurial spin-offs. Examples include:

- Ambient Clinical Analytics [bib#358] which "*sells clinical decision support systems and alerting tools to hospitals to reduce overall health care costs and improve patient outcomes*"; Mayo Clinic (Ventures) [bib#359]

- Centerline Biomedical [bib#360] which focuses on "*Intra-Operative Positioning System (IOPS™) technology — an innovative, non-x-ray based 3D GPS-like surgical navigation technology that improves endovascular procedure outcomes and reduces radiation exposure*"; Cleveland Clinic (Ventures) [bib#361]

- Navican [bib#362] "*was created to transform advances in precision medicine into precision cancer care for patients everywhere that advanced therapies are available*"; Intermountain Healthcare (Ventures) [bib#363]

Start-ups (usually a new organization not associated with any other – although sometimes a spin-off is referred to as a start-up – can start anywhere, but in the health and healthcare industry, they are often started in a start-up business incubator (sometimes called a business accelerator). Business Dictionary defines a business incubator [bib#364] as a:

> "*Facility established to nurture young (startup) firms during their early months or years. It usually provides affordable space, shared offices and services, hand-on management training, marketing support and, often, access to some form of financing.*"

There are many incubator facilities. Some of those focused on health and health care are listed in the:

- 12 healthcare startup incubators and accelerators to know [bib#365]
- Ultimate List of Medical Device Incubators and Accelerators (50+) [bib#366]
- Digital Health Accelerators [bib#367]
- Top 17 Health Startup Accelerators [bib#368]

Additional interesting resources on the topic are:

- How Healthcare Spin-Offs are Affecting the Industry [bib#369]
- The Top Resources For Healthcare Entrepreneurs, In Every Category. [bib#370]
- What is a pitch deck? [bib#371]
- Pitch Deck Examples [bib#372]
- Lessons From The Early Pitch Decks Of AirBnB, BuzzFeed, And YouTube [bib#373]
- 30 Legendary Startup Pitch Decks And What You Can Learn From Them [bib#374]

L2-T5. Business Plan

Every start-up and spin-off needs a business plan. Business Dictionary defines a business plan [bib#375] as:

"Set of documents prepared by a firm's management to summarize its operational and financial objectives for the near future (usually one to three years) and to show how they will be achieved. It serves as a blueprint to guide the firm's policies and strategies, and is continually modified as conditions change and new opportunities and/or threats emerge.

When prepared for external audience (lenders, prospective investors) it details the past, present, and forecasted performance of the firm. And usually also contains pro-forma balance sheet, income statement, and cash flow statement, to illustrate how the financing being sought will affect the firm's financial position."

The United States Small Business Administration (SBA) provides information, guidance, and templates for a business plan at its *Write your business plan* [bib#376] website. Although there is no one form of a business plan, according to the SBA:

A traditional business plan usually contains the following nine (9) sections:

1. Executive Summary
2. Company Description
3. Market Analysis
4. Organization And Management
5. Service or Product Line
6. Markcting and Sales
7. Funding Request
8. Financial Projections
9. Appendix

A lean start-up business plan usually contains the following nine (9) sections:

1. Key Partnerships
2. Key Activities
3. Key Resources
4. Value Proposition
5. Customer Relationships
6. Customer Segments
7. Channels
8. Cost Structure
9. Revenue Streams

Additional interesting resources on the topic are:

- 7 Steps to a Perfectly Written Business Plan [bib#377]
- How to Write the Perfect Business Plan: A Comprehensive Guide [bib#378]
- What is the Difference Between a Business Plan and a Strategic Plan? [bib#379]
- Pitch Deck vs. Business Plan: The Differences and Uses of Each [bib#380]

L2 Discussion Question: Disruptive Innovation in Healthcare

What, in your opinion, have been the most disruptive innovations in healthcare in the last 100 years? Are there, in your opinion, any disruptive innovations currently in process in healthcare?

L2 Quiz and "Create Your Own Healthcare Organization Business Processes"

L2 Quiz

Question 1

A _____ point is a place in the Business Process Flow where measurements are taken and evaluated against benchmarks to ensure that the business process is functioning as intended and whether a re-evaluation of the process is needed.

The answer to this question is found in Topic 1 and in the Lesson Two L2 Quiz Answer Key at the end of the Lesson Two L2 Quiz.

Question 2

ABPD software records and examines the "*electronic footprints the users leave in the IT assets supporting the process ... delivers the ability to take system data and automatically piece together 'as-is' business processes.*" ABPD stands for:

A. Analogous Business Production Data
B. Automated Business Process Discovery
C. Automated Broadcast Process Discovery
D. Actionable Belated Process Disruption

The answer to this question is found in Topic 1 and in the Lesson Two L2 Quiz Answer Key at the end of the Lesson Two L2 Quiz.

Question 3

Business Process Management Lifecycle is generally considered to have five (5) phases/components. Which of the following is **NOT** one of those phases/components?

A. Unleashing
B. Monitoring
C. Optimization

D. Optimization

The answer to this question is found in Topic 1 and in the Lesson Two L2 Quiz Answer Key at the end of the Lesson Two L2 Quiz.

Question 4

Business _____ Re-engineering (BPR) as the: *"Thorough rethinking of all business processes, job definitions, management systems, organizational structure, work flow, and underlying assumptions and beliefs."*

The answer to this question is found in Topic 2 and in the Lesson Two L2 Quiz Answer Key at the end of the Lesson Two L2 Quiz.

Question 5

An incremental setup that focuses on tinkering with the existing processes to improve them which identifies the process bottlenecks and recommends changes in specific functionalities without fundamentally changing the process framework is called:

A. Bilateral Plenary Initiative (BPI)
B. Business Process Improvement (BPI)
C. Continuous Quality Questions (CQQ)
D. Business Production Ingenuity (BPI)

The answer to this question is found in Topic 2 and in the Lesson Two L2 Quiz Answer Key at the end of the Lesson Two L2 Quiz.

Question 6

Some argue that automating bad business processes only makes them work badly much more quickly. Therefore, bad business processes should not be automated, but obliterated through re-engineering of those processes.

A. True
B. False

The answer to this question is found in Topic 2 and in the Lesson Two L2 Quiz Answer Key at the end of the Lesson Two L2 Quiz.

Question 7

To be called an innovation, an idea must be replicable at an economical cost and must satisfy a specific need.

A. True
B. False

The answer to this question is found in Topic 3 and in the Lesson Two L2 Quiz Answer Key at the end of the Lesson Two L2 Quiz.

Question 8

In general, innovation is considered to be in one of three categories. Which of the following is **NOT** one of those categories?

A. Product/Technology Innovation
B. Business Model Innovation
C. Animated Innovation
D. Process Innovation

The answer to this question is found in Topic 3 and in the Lesson Two L2 Quiz Answer Key at the end of the Lesson Two L2 Quiz.

Question 9

The Cochrane Library publishes systematic reviews which often discuss possible innovations in health care delivery. Each systematic review: *"summarises the results of available carefully designed healthcare studies (controlled trials) and provides a high level of evidence on the effectiveness of healthcare interventions. Judgments may be made about the evidence and inform recommendations for healthcare."*

A. True
B. False

The answer to this question is found in Topic 3 and in the Lesson Two L2 Quiz Answer Key at the end of the Lesson Two L2 Quiz.

Question 10

The: "*1. Assignment of technological intellectual property, developed and generated in one place, to another through legal means such as technology licensing or franchising. 2. Process of converting scientific and technological advances into marketable goods or services.*" is a definition of:

A. Process disruption
B. Product adoption
C. Innovation diffusion
D. Technology transfer

The answer to this question is found in Topic 4 and in the Lesson Two L2 Quiz Answer Key at the end of the Lesson Two L2 Quiz.

Question 11

The "*Theory that every market has groups of customers who differ in their readiness and willingness to adopt a new product. And, that an innovative product spreads (diffuses) through a market not in one straight course but in successive, overlapping waves. Most populations show the following pattern in the adoption of new consumer goods: innovators (2 percent of population), early adopters (14 percent), early majority (34 percent), late majority (34 percent), and laggards (16 percent).*" is a definition of:

A. Product adoption
B. Process disruption
C. Technology transfer
D. Innovation diffusion

The answer to this question is found in Topic 4 and in the Lesson Two L2 Quiz Answer Key at the end of the Lesson Two L2 Quiz.

Question 12

The University and Small Business Patent Procedures Act of 1980 which allows the patents (and royalties from those patents) to belong to the organization (university, small business, non-profit) making the discovery/invention rather than the federal government because they are usually better than the federal government developing partnerships to commercialize discoveries/inventions (innovation) made with federal money is commonly called:

A. Bayh-Dole
B. Mendendez-Booker
C. Bush-Durgin
D. Graham-Rand

The answer to this question is found in Topic 4 and in the Lesson Two L2 Quiz Answer Key at the end of the Lesson Two L2 Quiz

Question 13

Disruptive innovations are innovations which – over time - tend to make existing technologies/organizations obsolete. For that reason, disruptive innovations usually originate in which kind of organizations?

A. Organizations with more than 5000 employees
B. Organizations on the East Coast of the United States
C. Organizations outside of existing organizations – in smaller organizations which grow and replace larger organizations
D. Organizations which are large and have existed for a long time

The answer to this question is found in Topic 5 and in the Lesson Two L2 Quiz Answer Key at the end of the Lesson Two L2 Quiz

Question 14

The "*capacity and willingness to develop, organize and manage a business venture along with any of its risks in order to make a profit*" is a definition of:

A. Sponsorship
B. Entrepreneurship
C. Sportsmanship
D. Mentorship

The answer to this question is found in Topic 5 and in the Lesson Two L2 Quiz Answer Key at the end of the Lesson Two L2 Quiz.

<u>Question 15</u>

The "*Set of documents prepared by a firm's management to summarize its operational and financial objectives for the near future (usually one to three years) and to show how they will be achieved ... And usually also contains pro-forma balance sheet, income statement, and cash flow statement, to illustrate how the financing being sought will affect the firm's financial position.*" is a definition of a:

A. Research and Development Plan
B. Strategic Architectural Plan
C. Process Plan
D. Business Plan

The answer to this question is found in Topic 5 and in the Lesson Two L2 Quiz Answer Key at the end of the Lesson Two L2 Quiz.

L2 Quiz Answer Key

Q1 = control; Q2 = B; Q3 = A; Q4 = Process; Q5 = B; Q6 = A; Q7 = A; Q8 = C; Q9 = A; Q10 = D; Q11 = D; Q12 = A; Q13 = C; Q14 = B; Q15 = D

L2 "Create Your Own Healthcare Organization Business Processes"

In *Lesson Four*, you will *Design Healthcare Organization Business Processes*. This task requires that you synthesize content to create your own patient-centered business processes within a healthcare organization the way you would have things run in the best of all worlds. The type of healthcare organization is your choice (e.g., physical therapy office, dentist office, pharmacy, hospital, doctor's office).

It is suggested that your synthesized information be presented (formatted/designed) as a memo developed using word processing software (e.g., Microsoft Word). An example of a completed memo project is found in

Appendix B: Memo Example. The memo is an artifact of the book which you can circulate to colleagues or use for a talk or presentation event. For the suggested memo project, you will need word processing software. There are many software options. Some are available at no cost such as Writer [bib#211] which is part of LibreOffice [bib#212].

Nine (9) content items and seven (7) format/design items are suggested for the electronic memo task to develop competency.   However, it is best not to wait until Lesson Four to begin to synthesize content to create your own business processes for a healthcare organization. The earlier in your learning path that you begin this creation process, the better your own business processes within a healthcare organization will be.

So in each lesson prior to Lesson Four, there will be an opportunity to begin to synthesize material – an opportunity to begin to create your own business processes within a healthcare organization using material presented in that lesson. Of the nine (9) suggested content items for the completed memo, two (2) are suggested for consideration in this lesson. Each of the two is posted below and includes an expanded description as well as an example. They are:

Suggested Memo Content Item 7
> A brief description of the business processes used in your healthcare organization to stay current with innovations relevant to your healthcare organization. Also briefly state which innovation area is the one in which you expect to see the most innovation in the next five to ten years.
>
> *There are three broad innovation areas: 1) Product/Technology Innovation – bringing a new product/technology or an existing product with new technology to market (produced at scale at a reasonable cost which meets a consumer need); 2) Process Innovation – a new method/process for producing products at scale and at a reasonable cost; 3) Business Model Innovation - a new method (a new business model) for selling a product to consumers. There is no right or wrong answer to this question. It just has to be reasoned and make sense.*
>
> **Example:** CHGH provides financial support to employees to attend conferences, vendor demonstrations, and networking events in innovation

topic areas relevant to their workplace focus. Every six months CHGH asks for input from all employees regarding innovations not currently used by CHGH, but which should be used by CHGH. This input is organized by our CHGH Office of Innovation and distributed in a newsletter to all employees. The material in this newsletter is also discussed at a biannual meeting of all department chairs where decisions are made regarding which innovations to implement at CHGH. CHGH expects the most activity innovation to be in the area of Product/Technology Innovation.

Suggested Memo Content Item 8

A brief description of your healthcare organization's relationship to entrepreneurship. That is, does your organization actively seek to generate spin-off companies? Why or why not? If yes, are there organizational business processes to support it?

There is no right or wrong answer to this question. It just has to be reasoned and make sense.

Example: CHGH encourages all employees to have an entrepreneurial attitude. All employees are encouraged to take their innovation ideas and work to the CHGH Office of Innovation. Personnel from the Office of Innovation also try and maintain routine contact with all CHGH employees to encourage entrepreneurship and innovation. The Office of Innovation has business processes in place to try and turn CHGH employee innovation ideas into spin-off companies.

L2 Trivia Question and Virtual Field Trip

L2 Trivia Question

Almost everyone loves a trivia question – a question about a little known, but interesting, fun fact. Each lesson has one trivia question. The answer is in the Lesson Two Trivia Question Answer section.

Question:

The invention of the data storage device called "ticker tape [bib#381]" revolutionized the New York Stock Exchange (NYSE [bib#382]) and made ticker tape parades [bib#383] possible. Many devices were developed to produce useful ticker tape [bib#384]. One such device, called the Universal Stock Printer, was invented by a man whose company would evolve into the current General Electric Company. *Who is this inventor?*

L2 Trivia Question Answer

The answer to the Lesson Two trivia question is:

Thomas A. Edison

Thomas Edison introduced his Universal Stock Ticker [bib#385] in 1871. It was an improvement over the first stock ticker invented by Edward Calahan [bib#386] in 1867. Edison established the Edison General Electric Company in 1890. Edison was a great believer in "power naps [bib#387]" and he would take them throughout the day, often on the cot set up in his laboratory library.

For more information, please see:

- Thomas Edison & The History of Electricity [bib#388]
- Thomas A. Edison Papers [bib#389]
- Thomas Edison, Wikipedia [bib#390]
- 37 Quotes From Thomas Edison That Will Inspire Success [bib#391]

L2 Virtual Field Trip

Everyone loves a road trip/field trip so each lesson includes a "*virtual field trip*" to the often hidden places of interest on the web.

Lesson Two's virtual field trip is to the Thomas Edison National Historical Park [bib#392] in West Orange, New Jersey. The Park consists of

Edison's Laboratory [bib#393] as well as his nearby home which was named Glenmont [bib#394] Edison's Laboratory is also designated a National Historic Chemical Landmark [bib#395]by the American Chemical Society (ACS) because:

"*chemical applications were a central theme in many of his inventions ... When completed in 1887, the West Orange complex was the most modern and well-equipped industrial research facility in the world. It included several specialty laboratories for electricity, physics, chemistry, and metallurgy, as well as chemical storage and a library of chemical information to support Edison's expansive research. Over the next several decades as his inventions spawned industries, Edison established chemical manufacturing operations and factories nearby.*"

*****

Video [bib#396]: *The video for the Lesson Two Virtual Field Trip –* **Thomas Edison National Historical Park Educational Video** *– is a YouTube video produced by the Thomas Edison National Historical Park which provides a brief tour around Edison's Laboratory and a brief overview of Edison's life. The link for the video is:*
https://www.youtube.com/watch?v=Cf_0L0nIhrI

*****

Lesson Three (L3): Healthcare Organization Electronic Patient/Customer Records Business Processes

Note: The above picture is adapted from the one by the National Cancer Institute found on Unsplash (https://images.unsplash.com/photo-1576091160550-2173dba999ef?ixlib=rb-1.2.1&ixid=eyJhcHBfaWQiOjEyMDd9&auto=format&fit=crop&w=750&q=80)

L3 Competency Objective

This lesson provides an overview of healthcare organization electronic patient/customer records business processes. The competency objective is:

- Define healthcare organization electronic patient/customer records business processes.

L3 Content and Discussion

This lesson provides an overview of healthcare organization electronic patient/customer records business processes. Upon successful completion of this lesson, you will be able to: define healthcare organization electronic patient/customer records business processes. There are topic questions, a discussion question, a quiz, a trivia question, and a field trip. The lesson should take 4 - 6 hours of work to successfully complete. There are also videos which provide supplemental content which can help you better define your personal learning path. There are many wonderful videos in the public domain which are relevant to the topics in this book.

This lesson addresses five (5) topics organized as questions. The questions/topics for Lesson Three are:

1. What are Electronic Health Record (EHR) business processes for healthcare organizations?

2. What are Electronic Medical Record (EMR) business processes for healthcare organizations?

3. What are electronic pharmacy/medication business processes for healthcare organizations?

4. What are Electronic Dental Record (EDR) business processes for healthcare organizations?

5. What are Personal Health Record (PHR) business processes for healthcare organizations?

L3 Topic 1 (T1). What are Electronic Health Record (EHR) business processes for healthcare organizations?

There are many business processes involved in the implementation and use of an Electronic Health Record (EHR). Some people use the terms Electronic Health Record (EHR) and Electronic Medical Record (EMR) interchangeably, but many in the healthcare industry – including the Office of the National Coordinator for Health Information Technology (ONC [bib#397]) make a distinction between [bib#398]the two terms.

This section addresses:

- Difference Between an EHR and an EMR
- Types of Data Exchange in an EHR
- Interoperability
- HITECH and Meaningful Use
- Patient/Consumer Data Privacy

L3-T1. Difference Between EHR and EMR

The Office of the National Coordinator for Health Information Technology (ONC [bib#397]), founded in 2004, is:

> *"at the forefront of the administration's health IT efforts and is a resource to the entire health system to support the adoption of health information technology and the promotion of nationwide health information exchange to improve health care. ONC is organizationally located within the Office of the Secretary for the U.S. Department of Health and Human Services (HHS). ONC is the principal federal entity charged with coordination of nationwide efforts to implement and use the most advanced health information technology and the electronic exchange of health information. "*

ONC [bib#397] makes a clear distinction between [bib#229] an Electronic Health Record (EHR) and an Electronic Medical Record (EMR).

The ONC defines an Electronic Medical Record (EMR) as:

> *"a digital version of the paper charts in the clinician's office. An EMR contains the medical and treatment history of the patients in one practice … But the information in EMRs doesn't travel easily out of the practice. In fact, the patient's record might even have to be printed out and delivered by mail to specialists and other members of the care team. In that regard, EMRs are not much better than a paper record."*

The Office of the National Coordinator for Health Information Technology (ONC) defines an Electronic Health Record (EHR) as one which focuses:

> *"on the total health of the patient—going beyond standard clinical data collected in the provider's office and inclusive of a broader view on a patient's care. EHRs are designed to reach out beyond the health organization that originally collects and compiles the information. They are built to share information with other health care providers, such as laboratories and specialists, so they contain information from all the clinicians involved in the patient's care. The information moves with the patient—to the specialist, the hospital, the nursing home, the next state or even across the country."*

In short, the EMR is a patient's electronic record at one medical practice. That EMR can only be accessed by the members of that one medical practice. Sometimes patients are also allowed access to their own records. If a patient sees clinicians at multiple medical practices, then the patient will have multiple EMRs – one at each practice. The EHR, on the other hand, is the patient's complete electronic health record containing all health information – information from all of the EMRs and other health-related electronic records (e.g., laboratory test results, medications purchased, physical therapy treatments, dental treatments, FitBit tracking). The EHR is envisioned as being accessible by the patient as well as all those involved in the patient's health care.

Some envision the EHR as also containing evidence-based tools which can be used by health care delivery professionals to make health care delivery decisions. Others envision being able to analyze EHR data to determine patterns which might improve diagnosis and treatment.

L3-T1. Types of Data Exchange in an EHR

The EHR is the primary concern of the Office of the National Coordinator for Health Information Technology (ONC) which publishes the *Health IT Playbook* [bib#399]. The EHR is made possible by the sharing (exchange) of data maintained in different electronic databases – there is not one large EHR database into which a person's health data are transferred and stored. Instead, the data are maintained by the person/organization which "created" the data (e.g., the data for each EMR is stored in each medical practice organization's database) and shared (exchanged) with other healthcare organizations and health care delivery professionals, as needed, as well as the patient/consumer whose information it i

The ONC defines three major data exchange [bib#400] categories:

- Directed Exchange: 1) health care delivery professionals directly send and receive specific, secure electronic data (e.g., specific patient's laboratory test results) in support of coordinated health care delivery for a specific patient (two or more health care professionals in the EHR network share electronic data about a specific patient to coordinate the care of a patient being seen by both health care delivery professionals); and 2) health care delivery professionals directly send and receive specific, secure electronic data in reference to reimbursement from a third-party (e.g., insurance company) for a specific patient.

- Query-based Exchange: Health care delivery professionals find and/or request electronic data on a specific patient from other health care delivery professionals, often used for unplanned or emergency care (a health care professional in the EHR network checks to see if data about a specific patient exists in the EHR network for use in the health care of a patient about whom that health care delivery professional knows little).

- Consumer Mediated Exchange: Patients/consumers access, aggregate, and manage their health and health care delivery electronic data contained in the EHR network. For example, patient/consumers access laboratory test results, transfer data to a health care delivery professional, or correct inaccurate billing information.

In short, those with a need-to-know are able to easily access the needed data from any electronic health record which exists for a patient in the EHR network and/or receive an electronic copy of the needed data from another health record. The electronic data from all of the sources can be easily combined

– joined – to develop a more complete health picture for a patient. The key requirement for this to happen is that it is possible to exchange electronic data across the various participants in the EHR – this is often called interoperability.

L3-T1. Interoperability

Interoperability is one of the main concerns of the Office of the National Coordinator for Health Information Technology (ONC) because interoperability [bib#401] is central to a functioning EHR. The ONC:

"promotes the adoption and use of standards and technologies that allow health information to be shared electronically between clinicians, patients, researchers, and others with the authorization to the access the information. By promoting this ability to share information, often referred to as "interoperability," ONC aims to promote better care for patients, encourage stronger patient engagement in their own care, and lay the foundation for important new health initiatives, including the Precision Medicine Initiative."

The Precision Medicine Initiative (PMI) [bib#402]:

" launched in 2015, is a nationwide initiative to move away from the "one-size-fits-all" approach to health care delivery and to instead tailor treatment and prevention strategies to people's unique characteristics, including environment, lifestyle, and biology."

Specific Office of the National Coordinator for Health Information Technology (ONC) activities related to the PMI are participation in the Sync for Science (S4S) [bib#403] and Sync for Genes (S4G) [bib#404]. Both of these activities are in support of the All of Us Research Program [bib#405] which:

"is a historic effort to gather data over many years from one million or more people living in the United States, with the ultimate goal of accelerating research and improving health. Unlike research studies that are focused on a specific disease or population, All of Us will serve as a national research resource to inform thousands of studies,

covering a wide variety of health conditions. Researchers will use data from the program to learn more about how individual differences in lifestyle, environment, and biological makeup can influence health and disease. Participants may be able to learn more about their own health and contribute to an effort that may advance the health of generations to come."

The building blocks of interoperability are standards for both the data (vocabulary) and the technology used to electronically store and exchange the data. An example of a data standard is the use of SNOMED-CT [bib#406] for clinical vocabulary. An example of a technology standard is Health Level Seven (HL7) [bib#407]. A complete list of all the current standards (and there are many) can be found at HealthIT.gov Interoperability Standards Advisory (ISA [bib#408]) website, especially the ISA Reference Edition [bib#409].

*****

> **Video** [bib#410]: *The video for Topic 1 – **Introduction to HL7 and Interfaces in Healthcare** – is a YouTube video produced by LearnHealth Tech.* The video *provides an overview of what an interface is in Healthcare IT as well as some information about HL7 and interface engines. The link for the video is:*
> https://www.youtube.com/watch?v=T6dZOPHe2Jc

*****

Additional interesting resources on the topic are:

- ONC Interoperability Basics [bib#411]
- ONC Interoperability Roadmap [bib#412]
- Electronic health records: What will it take to make them work? [bib#413]

L3-T1. HITECH and Meaningful Use

The federal government has developed incentives for those involved in health care delivery to become part of an EHR network. A cornerstone of this effort was the 2009 Health Information Technology for Economic and Clinical Health (HITECH [bib#414]) Act which:

"proposes the meaningful use of interoperable electronic health records throughout the United States health care delivery system as a critical national goal. Meaningful Use is defined by the use of certified EHR technology in a meaningful manner (for example electronic prescribing)".

As a result of HITECH, the Centers for Medicare & Medicaid Services (CMS) offers incentive payments to encourage those clinicians receiving Medicare payments/reimbursements to use technology capable of EHR – this program has been called the EHR Incentive Program and the Meaningful Use Program, but is now called the Promoting Interoperability (PI [bib#415]) Program.

As part of this incentive program (which will likely become a penalty-for-non-use program over time), CMS released what are called Meaningful Use Stage 1, Stage 2, and Stage 3 requirements for the receipt of the incentives to encourage use of EHR technology.

- Meaningful Use (MU) Stage 1, which began in 2010, promotes the adoption of EMRs with EHR capability.

- Meaningful Use (MU) Stage 2, which began in 2012 and was modified in 2015, expands the EMR and EHR requirements.

- Meaningful Use (MU) Stage 3, which began in 2017, expands even further the EMR and EHR requirements.

Participation in the incentive program is currently voluntary, but it is expected that the incentives will become a mandatory penalty-for-non-use program over time. Healthcare organizations can demonstrate compliance with many of the requirements through use of Certified EHR Technology (CEHRT). Such technology is certified by the Office of the National Coordinator for Health

Information Technology (ONC) through its Health IT Certification Program [bib#416] which: "*provides assurance to purchasers and other users that a system meets the technological capability, functionality, and security requirements adopted by HHS*".

Additional interesting resources on the topic are:

- CMS Stage 1 MU Final Rule [bib#417]
- ONC Stage 1 MU Final Rule [bib#418]
- CMS Stage 2 MU Final Rule [bib#419]
- ONC Stage 2 MU Final Rule [bib#420]
- CMS Modified Stage 2 and Stage 3 Final Rule [bib#421]
- ONC Modified Stage 2 and Stage 3 Final Rule [bib#422]
- ONC Interoperability Training Courses [bib#423]
- ONC Tech Lab's Interoperability in Action Webinar Series [bib#424]

L3-T1. Patient/Consumer Data Privacy

The privacy of patient/consumer data has two aspects: 1) that patient/consumer data are stored and exchanged securely and only authorized access to the data occurs; and 2) that the patient/consumer is able to decide who sees the data and who does not (that the patient/consumer can keep some data private; that patient/consumer consent is required before the exchange of data).

The first situation depends on the security of the technology as well as federal, state, and local laws governing the use of patient/consumer data. The main federal law affecting the privacy and security of patient/consumer data is the Health Insurance Portability and Accountability Act [bib#425] of 1996 (HIPAA). The issues are addressed in some detail at the HealthIT.gov Privacy, Security, and HIPAA [bib#426] website.

The second situation has to do with patient/consumer consent for the data to be shared/exchanged with other healthcare professionals. This aspect is addressed in some detail at the HealthIT.gov Patient Consent for Electronic Health Information Exchange [bib#427] website as well as the HealthIT.gov

Patent Consent for Electronic Health Information Exchange and Interoperability [bib#428] website.

Additional interesting resources on the topic are:

- Health Information Exchange: What do patients want? [bib#429] (Abstract Only)
- Who Owns Health Information? [bib#430]
- Who Really Owns Your Health Data? [bib#431]

L3 Topic 2 (T2). What are Electronic Medical Record (EMR) business processes for healthcare organizations?

There are many business processes involved in the implementation and use of an Electronic Medical Record (EMR). As stated in Topic 1: The Office of the National Coordinator for Health Information Technology (ONC) defines an Electronic Medical Record (EMR) as:

"a digital version of the paper charts in the clinician's office. An EMR contains the medical and treatment history of the patients in one practice ... But the information in EMRs doesn't travel easily out of the practice. In fact, the patient's record might even have to be printed out and delivered by mail to specialists and other members of the care team. In that regard, EMRs are not much better than a paper record."

In short, the EMR is a patient's electronic record at one medical practice. That EMR can only be accessed by the members of that one medical practice. Sometimes patients are allowed access to their own records. If a patient sees clinicians at multiple medical practices, then the patient will have multiple EMRs – one at each practice.

This section addresses:

- Overview of the EMR
- EMR Implementation

L3-T2. Overview of the EMR

The invention of the medical record is generally credited to Henry Stanley Plummer [bib#432] at the Mayo Clinic in 1907. The first person to use computing in healthcare is generally considered to be Homer R. Warner [bib#433] with his work, starting in the mid-1950s, to develop computer-assisted decision-support systems in cardiology. This work resulted in a computer system named HELP (Health Evaluation through Logical Processing). The Homer Warner Center for Informatics Research [bib#434] at Intermountain Medical Center is named after him.

*****

> *Video* [bib#435]: *The video for Topic 2 – **Intermountain Medical Center: Homer Warner Center for Informatics Research** – is a YouTube video produced by IntermtnMedCtr. The video provides an overview of the work at the Homer Warner Center for Informatics Research. The link for the video is:* https://www.youtube.com/watch?v=t45AN-AgOgM

*****

The first electronic medical record (EMR) is generally credited to the Regenstrief Institute [bib#436] in 1972 when Clement McDonald [bib#437] and associates developed the Regenstrief Medical Record System.

The medical record is currently the basis for the medical coding used for analysis, reporting, and billing. Medical coding is the assignment of standardized codes to a patient's medical information. The first medical coding system is generally considered to be the one used with the London Bills of Mortality [bib#438] (weekly mortality statistics in London) begun in 1592.

The first comprehensive list of codes for medical conditions is generally considered to be the Bertillon List of Causes of Death [bib#439] (also known as the Bertillon Classification of the Causes of Death) first introduced in

1893. The work was largely spearheaded by Jacques Bertillon [bib#440], Chief of Statistical Services for the City of Paris. Through his efforts as well as those of the International Statistical Institute (ISI [bib#441]) and the American Public Health Association (APHA [bib#442]), the *Bertillon List of Causes of Death* was used throughout the world by 1899. In 1900, it was renamed the International List of Causes of Death [bib#443] and revised (referred to as ICD-1).

ISI had responsibility for the list and its revisions until ICD-6 in 1948 when the responsibility was transferred [bib#444] to the World Health Organization (WHO). In 1955, the name of the list was changed to its current International Classification of Diseases. The current version in use is ICD-10. A version ICD-11, however, has been developed.

The International Classification of Diseases (ICD) as implemented in the United States [bib#445] is the responsibility of the National Center for Health Statistics (NCHS [bib#446]) which is a division of the Centers for Disease Control and Prevention (CDC [bib#447]).

The assignment of standardized codes to data contained in the medical record is usually the job of a medical coder. In addition to ICD codes, medical coders also assign codes from other classification systems such as the: 1) Healthcare Common Procedure Coding System (HCPCS) Level II [bib#448] developed and maintained by the Centers for Medicare and Medicaid Services (CMS [bib#449]); and 2) Current Procedural Terminology (CPT [bib#450]) maintained by the American Medical Association (AMA [bib#451]). The HCPCS Level II code set and the CPT code set are each used to bill for clinical services and procedures.

Most medical coders are certified. Certification is available from the American Academy of Professional Coders (AAPC [bib#452]) which offers many medical coding and billing certifications [bib#453] including Certified Professional Coder (CPC [bib#454]). Certification is also available from the American Health Information Management Association (AHIMA [bib#455]) which also offers many certifications [bib#456] including the Certified Coding Specialist (CCS [bib#457]). The Practice Management Institute (PMI) [bib#458] also offers certifications [bib#459] including the Certified Medical Coder (CMC [bib#460]).

L3-T2. EMR Implementation

Incentives to participate in an Electronic Health Record (EHR) were briefly discussed in Topic 1. Any incentive to participate in an EHR is an incentive to use an EMR - there is no EHR without EMRs. In addition to EMR incentives, there are resources and toolkits for those who wish to implement an EMR.

One resource is the HealthIT.gov Workflow Process Mapping for Electronic Health Record (EHR) Implementation [bib#461] is:

> *"intended to aid providers and health IT implementers while planning for EHR implementation. The path to successful EHR implementation starts with practice workflow analysis and redesign. While this process isn't easy and takes time, efficiently managed workflow redesign can be the difference-maker to maximize office efficiencies and improve care coordination using EHRs. In fact, a lack of thorough workflow planning is one of the biggest reasons for avoidable losses in productivity and extended work days."*

Another resource is the HealthIT.gov Practice Transformation Toolkit [bib#462] which:

> *"is a comprehensive set of tools and resources that providers and staff members can use to implement a new or upgraded electronic health record (EHR) in order to transform and improve their practice in the areas of operations, clinical quality, finances, and staff and patient satisfaction. The Toolkit will not eliminate the challenges related to making such a large technology change.*
>
> *However, the Toolkit will provide a roadmap based upon best practices methodologies for EHR implementations and evaluations for successful transformation. The Toolkit allows a practice to avoid*

*making some fairly common mistakes, such as, purchasing EHR
products and services that do not meet the practice's expectations
and needs, or creating unrealistic timelines and expectations related
to the EHR implementation.*"

One of the best known EMR implementations is the Veterans
Information Systems and Technology Architecture (VISTA [bib#463] or VistA)
which:

*"consists of 180 applications for clinical, financial, and
administrative functions all integrated within a single database,
providing single, authoritative source of data for all veteran-related
care and services.*"

VistA was developed within the Department of Veterans Affairs and, as such, is
public domain.

VistA software documentation can be found at the VA Software
Document Library [bib#464] website. VistA modules and additional information
are available for download at WorldVistA [bib#465] and were available from
Open Source Electronic Health Record Alliance (OSEHRA [bib#466]) before
OSEHRA shut down in February 2020. In June 2017, it was announced that the
Department of Veterans Affairs would no longer support and use VistA.
However, WorldVistA continues:

*"to extend and collaboratively improve the VistA electronic health
record and health information system for use outside of its original
setting ... WorldVistA has a number of development efforts aimed at
adding new software modules such as pediatrics, obstetrics, and
other functions not used in the veterans' healthcare setting.*"

Before OSEHRA shut down in February 2020 and transferred all of its
resources it sought to:

*"Build and support an open source community of users, developers,
service providers, and researchers engaged in advancing electronic
health record software and related health information technology. "*

OSEHRA's mission includes the creation of a vendor-neutral community for the creation, evolution, promotion and support of an open source Electronic Health Record."

The Department of Veterans Affairs stopped developing and supporting VistA because the decision was made to replace VistA [bib#467] with the same system used by the Department of Defense (DoD). The new system is MHS Genesis [bib#468] which is based in Cerner's Millennium [bib#469] platform which is just one part of the Cerner offerings for Hospitals & Health Systems [bib#470].

Although the intent of the EMR is to facilitate workflow not all doctors are convinced. Some say that the EMR is more of a tool for billing and reporting rather than for direct care. There are doctors who say that use of EMRs actually hurts [bib#471] the physician-patient experience and relationship.

Additional interesting resources on the topic are:

- Poll: Doctors say electronic health records need overhaul [bib#472]

- DoD and VA Update: Early Results, Fine-tuning and Next Steps [bib#473]

- Measuring Performance Directly Using the Veterans Health Administration Electronic Medical Record: A Comparison With External Peer Review [bib#474]

- Utilizing patient data from the veterans administration electronic health record to support web-based clinical decision support: informatics challenges and issues from three clinical domains [bib#475]

- What Health Systems, Hospitals, and Physicians Need to Know About Implementing Electronic Health Records [bib#476]
- Kareo Go Practice Demo EMR/EHR Videos [bib#477]

- OpenEMR Demos [bib#478]

L3 Topic 3 (T3). What are electronic pharmacy/medication business processes for healthcare organizations?

There are many business processes associated with patient/customer medications. These business processes occur in the medication prescriber's office, in the transmission of the prescription information from the prescriber to the pharmacist, and in the pharmacy.

This section addresses:

- Electronic Business Processes for Medication Prescription
- Electronic Business Processes for Prescription Transmission
- Electronic Business Processes in the Pharmacy
- Electronic Medication Business Processes and the Opioid Epidemic

L3-T3. Electronic Business Processes for Medication Prescription

The 1970 federal Controlled Substances Act [bib#479] created five categories (schedules) for drugs in the United States and gave the United States Drug Enforcement Division (DEA) the authority to place [bib#480] a drug into one of the five categories. Each drug is classified according to the "drug's acceptable medical use and the drug's abuse or dependency potential".

- Schedule I drugs, substances, or chemicals are defined as drugs with no currently accepted medical use and a high potential for abuse (e.g., heroin).

- Schedule II drugs, substances, or chemicals are defined as drugs with a high potential for abuse, with use potentially leading to severe psychological or physical dependence. These drugs are also considered dangerous (e.g., OxyContin).

- Schedule III drugs, substances, or chemicals are defined as drugs with a moderate to low potential for physical and psychological dependence.

Schedule III drugs abuse potential is less than Schedule I and Schedule II drugs but more than Schedule IV (e.g., Tylenol with codeine).

- Schedule IV drugs, substances, or chemicals are defined as drugs with a low potential for abuse and low risk of dependence (e.g., Xanax).

- Schedule V drugs, substances, or chemicals are defined as drugs with lower potential for abuse than Schedule IV and consist of preparations containing limited quantities of certain narcotics (e.g., Robitussin AC).

Schedule I drugs are not legally available in the United States. Schedule II, III, and IV drugs are legally available with a prescription. Schedule V drugs are legally available without a prescription (over-the-counter). A prescription can only be legally ordered by a health care delivery professional with prescriptive authority. This authority is granted at the state level (health care delivery professionals are licensed at the state level). Doctors (MDs) in all states have prescriptive authority. Other health care delivery professionals in some states also have prescriptive authority (e.g., Nurse Practitioners, Physician Assistants, dentists for dental-related conditions).

Any ordered prescription is recorded in the patient's EMR, but the decision regarding which medication (prescription) to order is often complicated. The decision involves not only what is medically indicated for the patient, but also what acceptable medication has reasonable pricing for that patient. To help the health care delivery professional decide the optimal medication at the optimal price point for the patient (taking into consideration the patient's prescription drug plan, if any), electronic decision support systems which operate within and in conjunction with the EMR and the prescriber's workflow have been developed. Such systems are often called Real-Time Prescription Benefit (RTPB) and prior authorizations (PA) systems. Examples include, but are not limited to:

- RxBenefit Clarity [bib#481] which, when integrated into the physician's EMR/EHR for a patient, allows "*real-time pharmacy benefit coverage and price information for the patient during the physician's prescribing process ... to improve physician and pharmacy productivity – as well as patient adherence and satisfaction*". This is a product developed jointly by RelayHealth Pharmacy Solutions [bib#482] and CoverMyMeds [bib#483] which are both part of McKesson [bib#302].

- Two SureScripts [bib#484] products: Electronic Prior Authorization [bib#485] which "*integrates directly with electronic health records (EHRs), enabling healthcare professionals to easily obtain prior authorizations in real time at the point of care*" and Real-Time Prescription Benefit [bib#486] which "*delivers patient-specific drug benefit and cost information to the e-prescribing workflow at the point of care. Combined with Electronic Prior Authorization, this solution lets prescribers make medication decisions with full price transparency*".

- CVS Health [bib#487] through CVS Caremark [bib#488] offers electronic real-time prescription benefit decision support to prescribers, pharmacists, and patients/customers in the Caremark Network. It is a "*comprehensive initiative to make real-time, member-specific prescription benefit information available across all points of care ... enables prescribers to make better informed decisions and encourages the use of a clinically appropriate drug that may cost the plan member less ...help payors control costs by encouraging the use of clinically appropriate, lower-cost alternatives*".

Additional interesting resources on the topic are:

- DEA: The Controlled Substances Act [bib#489]
- FDA: Drugs [bib#490]

L3-T3. Electronic Business Processes for Prescription Transmission

Electronic business processes for prescription transmission are commonly called electronic prescribing or E-Prescribing. The Centers for Medicare and Medicaid Services (CMS) defines E-Prescribing [bib#491] as:

"a prescriber's ability to electronically send an accurate, error-free and understandable prescription directly to a pharmacy from the point-of-care - is an important element in improving the quality of patient care. The inclusion of electronic prescribing in the Medicare Modernization Act (MMA) of 2003 gave momentum to the movement, and the July 2006 Institute of Medicine report on the role of e-prescribing in reducing medication errors received widespread publicity, helping to build awareness of e-prescribing's role in enhancing patient safety."

The 2006 Institute of Medicine (IOM) report mentioned above is entitled Preventing Medication Errors: Quality Chasm Series [bib#492]. This report finds that by "*writing prescriptions electronically, doctors and other providers can avoid many of the mistakes that accompany handwritten prescriptions, as the software ensures that all the necessary information is filled out—and legible*".

Many E-Prescribing systems are built into other systems such as a Real-Time Prescription Benefit (RTPB) or prior authorizations (PA) system. One stand-alone system is MDtoolbox E-Prescribing [bib#493]. This system is EPCS compliant [bib#494] as must be all E-Prescribing systems for controlled substances. EPCS stands for Electronic Prescribing of Controlled Substances. The EPCS standards for compliance were first established by the Drug Enforcement Administration (DEA) in 2010 [bib#495].

Additional interesting resources on the topic are:

- E-Prescribing Enables Pharmacists to Improve Medication Adherence [bib#496]
- AAFP - Electronic Prescribing of Controlled Substances (EPCS) [bib#497]

L3-T3. *Electronic Business Processes in the Pharmacy*

Pharmacies have long maintained a Patient Medication Record (PMR) for each patient/customer who obtains prescription medications from that pharmacy. It is a list of the medications (and additional information such as dosage) obtained by that patient/customer at that pharmacy. There now exist electronic PMRs for record-keeping at one pharmacy (e.g., a stand-alone retail pharmacy) or any pharmacy in a particular network (e.g., one PMR for each person across all CVS pharmacies). Usually the PMR is part of a complete Pharmacy Management System [bib#498] and sometimes it can be purchased as a stand-alone system.

There is a growing interest in the expansion of the PMR into a record that more closely resembles the EMR for each pharmacy patient/customer largely because the services offered by pharmacists and pharmacies are expanding. For example, many retail pharmacies offer walk-in clinic services such as those found in a CVS Minute Clinic [bib#499] as well as disease management programs and support for those with chronic illnesses. An example of the latter situation is the CVS Health Transform Care [bib#500] program, specifically the CVS Health Transform Diabetes Care [bib#501] program and the CVS Health Transform Rheumatoid Arthritis Care [bib#502].

In addition, the Medicare Modernization Act (MMA) of 2003 required Medicare Part D prescription drug plans to require Medication Therapy Management (MTM) services to include a single record of all the patient's/customers medications, medication counseling, and medication coordination with prescribers. Much of such MTM services are done by pharmacies and pharmacists [bib#503]

L3-T3. Electronic Medication Business Processes and the Opioid Epidemic

Every day, more than 115 people [bib#504] in the United States die from an opioid overdose which is more than 40,000 people per year. An estimated 40% of opioid overdose deaths involved a prescription opioid [bib#505]. To help combat this opioid overdose epidemic, the *Substance Use-Disorder Prevention that Promotes Opioid Recovery and Treatment (SUPPORT* [bib#506]*) for Patients and Communities Act* (H.R.6) was signed into law in October 2018.

Some of the provisions of this law address and encourage the use of electronic pharmacy and medication systems such as: 1) E-Prescribing systems compliant with Electronic Prescribing of Controlled Substances (EPCS) standards; and 2) Prescription Drug Monitoring Program (PDMP [bib#507]) databases.

"PDMPs are one of the most promising tools available to address prescription opioid misuse and abuse. PDMPs are state-run electronic databases ... that collect data from pharmacies on controlled prescription drugs dispensed to patients. Pharmacists (and some dispensing physicians) report to a PDMP each time a prescription is filled for a controlled substance medication ...

PDMP information can give a prescriber or pharmacist critical information regarding a patient's controlled substance prescription history. This, in turn, can help providers distinguish between patients who legitimately need opioid medications for pain treatment and those who may be seeking to misuse or divert (i.e., channeling drugs into illegal use) these powerful drugs".

EPCS compliant E-Prescribing systems decrease the possibility of forged/altered opioid prescriptions and thus decrease the possibility of drug diversion (prescription drugs for illegal uses). It is estimated that between 3% and 9% of diverted drugs are tied to fraud or forgery of paper prescriptions.

*****

> **Video** [bib#508]: *The video for Topic 3 –* **The Science of Opioids** *– is a YouTube video produced by Healthcare Triage. The video provides an overview of the physiological processes that let opioids produce their effects in human bodies. The link for the video is:*
> https://www.youtube.com/watch?v=AqDo4LiKz-c

*****

Additional interesting resources on the topic are:

- Making Progress in the Fight Against Opioid Misuse and Abuse [bib#509]
- OPIOIDS [bib#510]
- Opioid Crisis [bib#511]
- Opioid Overdose [bib#512]
- Four Ways Pharmacists Are Fighting Opioid Abuse [bib#513]
- What States Need to Know about PDMPs [bib#514]
- Purdue Phama - Open Letter [bib#515]

L3 Topic 4 (T4). What are Electronic Dental Record (EDR) business processes for healthcare organizations?

There are many business processes involved in the implementation and use of an Electronic Dental Record (EDR). This section addresses:

- Overview of the EDR
- EDR Incentives and Examples

L3-T4. Overview of the EDR

The Office of the National Coordinator for Health Information Technology (ONC) definition of an Electronic Medical Record (EMR) can be adapted to describe the Electronic Dental Record (EDR). The EDR is:

a digital version of the paper charts in the dentist's office. An EDR contains the dental and treatment history of the patients in one practice ... But the information in EDRs doesn't travel easily out of the practice. In fact, the patient's record might even have to be printed out and delivered by mail to specialists and other members of the care team. In that regard, EDRs are not much better than a paper record.

In short, the EDR is a patient's electronic record at one medical practice. That EDR can only be accessed by the members of that one dental practice Sometimes patients are allowed access to their own records. If a patient sees dentists at multiple dental practices, then the patient will have multiple EDRs – one at each practice.

The EDR is similar to the EMR in all ways (e.g., same technology standards, same data standards) except it is tailored toward the data gathered and used in a dental practice rather than a medical practice (e.g., EDR contains a tooth chart).

It is estimated that more than 15 percent of dental practices [bib#516] in the United States use a full EDR (no paper records) while an additional 70 percent have a combination of paper and electronic dental records for patients/customer.

L3-T4. EDR Incentives and Examples

Some dental practices, when implementing an EDR, can take advantage of some of the incentives [bib#517] available at the federal level for EMR and Electronic Health Record (EHR) implementation. There may also be incentives at the state level for those dental practices which participate in Medicaid.

An EDR is usually contained within dental practice management software (rather than as a stand-alone EDR). Often the dental practice management software has Electronic Health Record (EHR) capability (interoperability). Examples include:

- ACE Dental [bib#518]
- Curve Dental [bib#519]
- iDental Soft [bib#520]
- Planet DDS Denticon [bib#521]
- Tab32 [bib#522]

Additional interesting resources on the topic are:

- American Dental Association (ADA): Electronic Health Records [bib#523]
- Weighing the Challenges and Benefits of Dental EHRs [bib#524]
- Clinical Documentation of Dental Care in an Era of EHR Use [bib#525]
- Five of the best dentistry EHRs [bib#526]
- Dental Software [bib#527]
- Dental Practice Software [bib#528]

*****

Video [bib#529]: *The video for Topic 4 – **Exploring the History of Teeth at Baltimore's Dentistry Museum** – is a YouTube video produced by VOA News. The video is a brief visit to the Dr. Samuel D. Harris National Museum of Dentistry* [bib#530] *at the University of Maryland School of Dentistry in Baltimore, Maryland. The link for the video i*s:
(https://www.youtube.com/watch?v=YHiPuRiKWwE

*****

L3 Topic 5 (T5). What are Personal Health Record (PHR) business processes for healthcare organizations?

Although the Personal Health Record (PHR) belongs to the patient/customer, all healthcare organizations must decide if they wish to devote business processes to the PHR. That is, does the healthcare organization wish to have business processes which support and encourage patients/customers to develop a PHR? Does the healthcare organization have business processes which allow the exchange of data between the healthcare organization and a patient's/customer's PHR?

Those in the healthcare industry who support the widespread use of PHRs often do so because of a belief that such Personal Health Records (PHRs) help patients/customers become more actively involved in their health care delivery - to become partners with the healthcare organization in their health care delivery. As such, healthcare organizations which devote business processes to the PHR could be considered to be more directed toward patient-centered health care delivery than those which do not.

This section addresses:

- Overview of the Personal Health Record (PHR)
- Personal Health Record (PHR) Examples

L3-T5. Overview of the Personal Health Record (PHR)

HealthIT.gov states that a Personal Health Record (PHR [bib#531]): "*is an electronic application through which patients can maintain and manage their health information (and that of others for whom they are authorized) in a private, secure, and confidential environment*" and that PHRs **[bib#532]**:

"*contain the same types of information as EHRs—diagnoses, medications, immunizations, family medical histories, and provider contact information—but are designed to be set up, accessed, and managed by patients. Patients can use PHRs to maintain and manage their health information in a private, secure, and confidential* environment. PHRs can include information from a variety of sources including clinicians, home monitoring devices, and patients themselves*."*

In general, PHRs can be divided into two types [bib#533]: Stand-Alone PHR and Tethered, Connected PHR.

- A Stand-Alone PHR is one maintained entirely by the patient/customer from personal records; that is "*patients fill in the information from their own records and memories and the data is stored on the patients' computers or on the internet. Patients can decide whether to share the information with providers, family members, or anyone else involved in their care. In some cases, information can be downloaded from other sources into the PHR.*"

- A Tethered, Connected PHR is one created by a patient/customer from the records of a healthcare organization; that is, it is "*linked to a specific health care organization's EHR system or a health plan's information system. The patient accesses the information through a secure portal. Typically, patients can view information such as lab results, immunization history or due dates for certain screenings. These are called tethered PHRs or connected PHRs. When a PHR is connected to the patient's legal medical record it is protected under the Health Insurance Portability and Accountability Act (HIPPA) Privacy Rule.*"

L3-T5. Personal Health Record (PHR) Examples

Examples of Stand-Alone PHRs can be found (and downloaded for use) at the American Health Information Management Association (AHIMA) MyPHR [bib#534] website, specifically the Choose a PHR [bib#535] website. The MyPHR video library [bib#536] website also provides useful information.

An example of a tethered, connected PHR is the Centers for Medicare and Medicaid Services (CMS) new MyHealthEData Initiative [bib#537] which seeks to strengthen interoperability and create a more patient-centered healthcare system. This Initiative [bib#538]:

 "*aims to empower patients by ensuring that they control their healthcare data and can decide how their data is going to be used, all while keeping that information safe and secure ... MyHealthEData will help to break down the barriers that prevent patients from having electronic access and true control of their own health records from the device or application of their choice. This effort will approach the issue of healthcare data from the patient's perspective.*"

One component [bib#539] of this Initiative is Medicare's Blue Button and Blue Button 2.0. Blue Button [bib#540] makes it easy for Medicare patients/customers to download their personal health information to a file on their personal computing device. Blue Button 2.0 [bib#541] allows Medicare patients/customers to connect (exchange) their Medicare data to other applications, services, and research programs, should they wish to do so.

Additional interesting resources on the topic are:

- What are the benefits of personal health records? [bib#542]
- Electronic Health Records Infographic [bib#543]
- Why consumers want their health records [bib#544]
- Electronic health records: What will it take to make them work? [bib#413]

*****

Video [bib#545]: *The video for Topic 5 – **MyHealthEData** – is a YouTube video produced by CMSHHSgov. The video is a brief overview of how MyHealthEData empowers patients by ensuring they control their healthcare data and can decide how their data is going to be used. The link for the video i*s: https://www.youtube.com/watch?v=2DCeCdU1PeE

*****

L3 Discussion Question: Exchange and Use of Your Personal Health Data

What is your opinion about how and when your personal health data contained in electronic records (e.g., Electronic Medical Record) can be exchanged and used? For example, do you want to be the one to make all data exchanges; that is, all requests go to you rather than your health care delivery professional? Can any of your personal health data created by your health care delivery professional be exchanged with other professionals?

L3 Quiz and "Create Your Own Healthcare Organization Business Processes"

L3 Quiz

Question 1

An Electronic _____ Record (EHR) is a record which focuses: "*on the total health of the patient—going beyond standard clinical data collected in the provider's office and inclusive of a broader view on a patient's care.*"

The answer to this question is found in Topic 1 and in the Lesson Three L3 Quiz Answer Key at the end of the Lesson Three L3 Quiz

Question 2

The Office of the National Coordinator for Health Information Technology (ONC) defines three major data exchange categories. Which of the following is **NOT** one of those categories?

A. Directed Exchange
B. Query-based Exchange
C. Consumer Medicated Exchange
D. Tollbooth Exchange

The answer to this question is found in Topic 1 and in the Lesson Three L3 Quiz Answer Key at the end of the Lesson Three L3 Quiz

Question 3

The ability to share health information electronically between clinicians, patients, researchers, and others with the authorization to access the information is often referred to as:

A. Security Scan
B. Innovation
C. Interoperability
D. Rebooting

The answer to this question is found in Topic 1 and in the Lesson Three L3 Quiz Answer Key at the end of the Lesson Three L3 Quiz.

Question 4

A digital version of the paper charts in the clinician's office which contains the medical and treatment history of the patients in one practice is called an:

A. Person Hospitalization Reminder (PHR)
B. Everyperson Medication Record (EMR)
C. Personal Health Record (PHR)
D. Electronic Medical Record (EMR)

The answer to this question is found in Topic 2 and in the Lesson Three L3 Quiz Answer Key at the end of the Lesson Three L3 Quiz.

Question 5

The path to successful Electronic Medical Record (EMR)/Electronic Health Record (EHR) implementation starts with practice workflow analysis and redesign ... efficiently managed workflow redesign can be the difference-maker to maximize office efficiencies and improve care coordination using EMRs/EHRs. In fact, a lack of thorough workflow planning is one of the biggest reasons for avoidable losses in productivity and extended work days.

A. True
B. False

The answer to this question is found in Topic 2 and in the Lesson Three L3 Quiz Answer Key at the end of the Lesson Three L3 Quiz.

Question 6

Although the intent of the Electronic Medical Record (EMR) is to facilitate workflow not all doctors are convinced. Some say that the EMR is more of a tool for billing and reporting rather than for direct care. There are doctors who say that use of EMRs actually hurts the physician-patient experience and relationship.

A. True
B. False

The answer to this question is found in Topic 2 and in the Lesson Three L3 Quiz Answer Key at the end of the Lesson Three L3 Quiz.

Question 7

Real-Time Prescription Benefit (RTPB) and prior authorizations (PA) systems are electronic decision support systems which operate within and in conjunction with the Electronic Medical Record (EMR) and the prescriber's workflow to:

A. Help the dentist decide whether to recommend an implant or not
B. Help the pharmacist decide which formulary to use
C. Help the health care delivery professional decide the optimal medication at the optimal price point for the patient (taking into consideration the patient's prescription drug plan, if any)
D. Help the patient/customer decide the optimal which health care delivery provider to use

The answer to this question is found in Topic 3 and in the Lesson Three L3 Quiz Answer Key at the end of the Lesson Three L3 Quiz.

Question 8

E-Prescribing can be defined as "*a prescriber's ability to electronically send an accurate, error-free and understandable prescription directly to a pharmacy from the point-of-care - is an important element in improving the quality of patient care."*

A. True
B. False

The answer to this question is found in Topic 3 and in the Lesson Three L3 Quiz Answer Key at the end of the Lesson Three L3 Quiz.

Question 9

Many believe that one of the most promising tools available to address prescription opioid misuse and abuse are state-run electronic databases ... that collect data from pharmacies on controlled prescription drugs dispensed to patients. These databases are part of the:

A. Controlled Substance Reporting System (CSRS)
B. Opioid Allowance Restriction Program (OARP)
C. Prescription Initiative Allowance Program (PIAP)
D. Prescription Drug Monitoring Program (PDMP)

The answer to this question is found in Topic 3 and in the Lesson Three L3 Quiz Answer Key at the end of the Lesson Three L3 Quiz.

Question 10

A digital version of the paper charts in the dentist's office which contains the dental and treatment history of the patients in one practice is usually called an:

A. Electronic Dentistry Production (EDP)
B. Tooth Processing System (TPS)
C. Electronic Dental Record (EDR)
D. Dentist Digital Image (DDI)

The answer to this question is found in Topic 4 and in the Lesson Three L3 Quiz Answer Key at the end of the Lesson Three L3 Quiz.

Question 11

It is estimated that more than 15 percent of dental practices in the United States use a full electronic record (no paper records) while an additional 70 percent have a combination of paper and electronic dental records for patients/customer.

A. True

B. False

The answer to this question is found in Topic 4 and in the Lesson Three L3 Quiz Answer Key at the end of the Lesson Three L3 Quiz.

Question 12

Some dental practices implementing an Electronic Dental Record (EDR) are eligible to take advantage of some of the incentives for the Electronic Medical Record (EMR) and Electronic Health Record (EHR) implementation at the federal and state levels.

A. True

B. False

The answer to this question is found in Topic 4 and in the Lesson Three L3 Quiz Answer Key at the end of the Lesson Three L3 Quiz.

Question 13

A Personal Health Record (PHR)is an electronic application through which patients can maintain and manage their health information (and that of others for whom they are authorized) in a private, secure, and confidential environment.

A. True

B. False

The answer to this question is found in Topic 5 and in the Lesson Three L3 Quiz Answer Key at the end of the Lesson Three L3 Quiz.

Question 14

In general, Personal Health Records (PHRs) can be divided into two types. Which of the following is **NOT** one of those types?

A. Summary, Defined PHR
B. Tethered, Connected PHR
C. Stand-Alone PHR

The answer to this question is found in Topic 5 and in the Lesson Three L3 Quiz Answer Key at the end of the Lesson Three L3 Quiz.

Question 15

The federal Initiative which seeks to strengthen interoperability and create a more patient-centered healthcare system by approaching the issue of healthcare data from the patient's perspective and breaking down the barriers that prevent patients from having electronic access and true control of their own health records from the device or application of their choice is called the:

A. Data Access Initiative
B. Personal Health Initiative
C. MyHealthEData Initiative
D. Centers for Disease Control and Prevention (CDC) Initiative

The answer to this question is found in Topic 5 and in the Lesson Three L3 Quiz Answer Key at the end of the Lesson Three L3 Quiz.

L3 Quiz Answer Key

Q1 = Health; Q2 = D; Q3 = C; Q4 = D; Q5 = A; Q6 = A; Q7 = C; Q8 = A; Q9 = D; Q10 = C; Q11 = A; Q12 = A; Q13 = A; Q14 = A; Q15 = C

L3 "Create Your Own Healthcare Organization Business Processes"

In *Lesson Four*, you will *Design Healthcare Organization Business Processes*. This task requires that you synthesize content to create your own patient-centered business processes within a healthcare organization the way you would have things run in the best of all worlds. The type of healthcare organization is your choice (e.g., physical therapy office, dentist office, pharmacy, hospital, doctor's office).

It is suggested that your synthesized information be presented (formatted/designed) as a memo developed using word processing software (e.g., Microsoft Word). An example of a completed memo project is found in *Appendix B: Memo Example*. The memo is an artifact of the book which you can circulate to colleagues or use for a talk or presentation event. For the suggested memo project, you will need word processing software. There are many software options. Some are available at no cost such as Writer [bib#211] which is part of LibreOffice [bib#212].

Nine (9) content items and seven (7) format/design items are suggested for the electronic memo task to develop competency. However, it is best not to wait until Lesson Four to begin to synthesize content to create your own business processes for a healthcare organization. The earlier in your learning path that you begin this creation process, the better your own business processes within a healthcare organization will be.

So in each lesson prior to Lesson Four, there will be an opportunity to begin to synthesize material – an opportunity to begin to create your own business processes within a healthcare organization using material presented in that lesson. Of the nine (9) suggested content items for the completed memo, one (1) is suggested for consideration in this lesson. It is posted below and includes an expanded description as well as an example. It is:

Suggested Memo Content Item 9

A brief description of the business processes used in your healthcare organization regarding electronic patient/customer records? For example, describe the extent to which your healthcare organization uses such software and for what purposes. If electronic patient/customer records are not used, why not? If electronic patient/customer records are used, are they Electronic Health Record (EHR) compatible? What is the relationship between your records and a patient's/customer's Personal Health Record (PHR)?

There is no right or wrong answer to this question. It just has to be reasoned and make sense.

Example: CHGH attempts to always use the most innovative Electronic Medical Record (EMR) available in the most cost-effective way. The CHGH Office of Technology is responsible for ensuring that the EMR functions well on a day-to-day basis as well as being the most up-to-date and in compliance with all mandated and recommended capabilities. The chosen EMR is EHR compliant. Patients/customers are able to access and download all EMR data to their PHR except the private clinical notes of health care delivery professionals. Patients/customers are also encouraged to upload any PHR data they wish exchange/share with CHGH.

L3 Trivia Question and Virtual Field Trip

L3 Trivia Question

Almost everyone loves a trivia question – a question about a little known, but interesting, fun fact. Each lesson has one trivia question. The answer is in the Lesson Three Trivia Question Answer section.

Question:

Before electronic calculators and computers, mathematical calculations were often done using a slide rule. *Who is generally credited with the basic original design of the slide rule?*

L3 Trivia Question Answer

The answer to the Lesson Three trivia question is:

William Oughtred

William Oughtred [bib#546] is credited with inventing the slide rule in 1622. He is also credited with the introduction of the "×" symbol for multiplication as well as the abbreviations "sin" and "cos" for the sine and cosine functions.

For more information, please see:

- William Oughtred, Wikipedia [bib#547]
- About Slide Rules [bib#548]
- Slide Rule, Wikipedia [bib#549]
- What Can You Do With A Slide Rule? [bib#550]
- The Slide Rule: A Computing Device That Put A Man On The Moon [bib#551]

L3 Virtual Field Trip

Everyone loves a road trip/field trip so each lesson includes a "*virtual field trip*" to the often hidden places of interest on the web.

Lesson Three's virtual field trip is to the Massachusetts Institute of Technology (MIT) Museum [bib#552] in Cambridge, Massachusetts. It is open to the public. The museum contains [bib#553]:

"*rich and diverse collections of art, artifacts, prints, rare books, technical archives, drawings, photographs and holograms dating from 7th century BCE to today. The collections reflect the diverse interests of the MIT Community from the founding in 1861, to current cutting edge research.*"

Also housed at the museum is the MIT Museum Studio [bib#554] which:

"*connects MIT undergraduate and graduate students with the unique learning opportunities of the MIT Museum ... the studio is a fully functional maker space and learning laboratory that supports the creation of student projects and installations ... Many of these student-generated installations are now displayed in the museum's galleries.*"

*****

Video [bib#555]: *The video for the Lesson Three Virtual Field Trip – **Slide Rules** – is a YouTube video produced by the MIT Alumni Association in collaboration* with the MIT Museum about MIT student familiarity with the slide rule. *The link for the video i*s:
https://www.youtube.com/watch?v=CblhxhnSymg

*****

Lesson Four (L4): Design Patient-Centered Healthcare Organization Business Processes

L4 Competency Objectives

This lesson is a synthesis of the book material to design patient-centered healthcare organization business processes the way you would have things run in the best of all worlds. The competency objectives are:

- Synthesize course content to create patient-centered business processes for a healthcare organization.

- Generate an effective memo suitable for discussion, presentation, and printing.

L4 Content and Discussion

This lesson is a synthesis of the book material to design and present patient-centered business processes in a healthcare organization the way you would have things run in the best of all worlds.

The purpose of this lesson is to help you improve your skills in presenting your point of view and arguing for your view of the best business processes in a healthcare organization

There are two topic sections, a discussion question, two self-evaluations, one electronic memo file creation, a trivia question, and a field trip. The electronic memo file is an artifact of the book's learning path which you can circulate to colleagues or use for a talk or presentation event. The lesson should take 4 - 6 hours of work to successfully complete. There are also videos which provide supplemental content which can help you better define your personal learning path. There are many wonderful videos in the public domain which are relevant to the topics in this book.

In constructing your memo, you are going to do so from the perspective of the chief healthcare administrator for your organization. You are describing your organization's patient-centered business processes to an audience.

Healthcare administration encompasses responsibility for all aspects of a healthcare organization. The focus is both internal to the organization and external to the organization to maximize the efficient and effective operation of the organization as a whole and its survival both short-term and long term. Healthcare administrators make decisions about the direction and operation of the healthcare organization. The role of the healthcare administrator is more strategic than tactical.

The two topics for Lesson Four are:

- Suggested content for the memo
- Suggested format for the memo

L4 Topic 1 (T1). Suggested content for the memo

The memo project suggests that you to synthesize course material to design patient-centered business processes for a healthcare organization the way you would have things run in the best of all worlds. The memo file is an artifact of the course which you can circulate to colleagues or use for a talk or presentation event. It is suggested that your synthesized information be presented (formatted/designed) as a memo developed using word processing software (e.g., Microsoft Word). There are many software options. Some are available at no cost such as Writer [bib#211] which is part of LibreOffice [bib#212]. An example of a completed memo project is found in *Appendix B: Memo Example*.

The nine (9) suggested memo content items were specified in the first three lessons. You can certainly add more content to your memo than the suggested nine (9) content items – or less. Each one of the suggested nine items is listed (once again) below with an example and the suggested self-evaluation rubric (evaluation criterion).

In the ***Lesson Four Self-Evaluations*** section is a "*quiz*" entitled ***Synthesize Content Self-Evaluation***. This quiz is a self-evaluation as to whether you have accomplished the synthesis of content described here. Not surprising, it is a nine (9) question quiz asking whether you have developed the nine suggested memo content items.

Suggested Memo Content Item 1: The name of your healthcare organization in which you will design your patient-centered health care delivery system?

- Example: Charles Harbor General Hospital (CHGH)

- *Evaluation Rubric: The name should be original and give some sense to healthcare consumers as to the healthcare products found in the organization.*

Suggested Memo Content Item 2: A brief description of your healthcare organization. What does your healthcare organization do?

- Example: Charles Harbor General Hospital (CHGH) is a private, non-profit, general hospital in Massachusetts. It has an emergency room and a full range of clinical specialties (e.g., internal medicine, general surgery, oncology, cardiology, infectious disease, pediatrics).

- *Evaluation Rubric: The description should be a few sentences which concisely and clearly summarize for healthcare consumers the type of healthcare organization, its location, and its products.*

Suggested Memo Content Item 3: A brief, broad overview of the most important Use Case for your patient-centered healthcare organization; that is, what are the most important requirements patients have for your healthcare organization?

- Example: CHGH patients want to feel confident in the health care they receive from CHGH; that, it patients want to have full confidence in the CHGH health care delivery personnel. Patients also want to feel respected and treated as individuals. Patients also want the facilities to be clean and comfortable.

- *Evaluation Rubric: The Use Case concept can be applied to a patient-centered healthcare organization's business processes regardless of whether the processes are automated. Such a Use Case describes how the patient/customer interacts with (views and uses) the healthcare organization's business processes. It describes the patient/customer requirements for doing business with the healthcare organization (what features does the patient/customer want). A Use Case provides a framework for the healthcare organization what the business processes are supposed to do (Use Case Business Process Management). There is no right or wrong answer to this question. It just has to be reasoned and make sense.*

<u>Suggested Memo Content Item 4:</u> A brief, broad overview of the Operational Business Processes most important to your Use Case.

- <u>Example:</u> For the CHGH Use Case requirements to be met, CHGH must have superior, patient-centered health care delivery personnel and excellent health care delivery facilities and equipment.

- *<u>Evaluation Rubric:</u> Operational Business Processes (sometimes called Core Business Processes or Primary Business Processes) are the processes which produce direct value for the customer; they produce the organization's product and often have direct contact with the organization's customer. In a healthcare organization, these processes are those related to health care delivery. There is no right or wrong answer to this question. It just has to be reasoned and make sense.*

<u>Suggested Memo Content Item 5:</u> A brief, broad overview of the Supporting Business Processes most important to your Use Case.

- <u>Example:</u> For the CHGH Use Case requirements to be met, CHGH must have superior human resources personnel and processes to ensure that the health care delivery personnel are superior and patient-centered. CHGH also needs superior facilities personnel and processes to ensure that health care delivery facilities and equipment are superior, clean, and comfortable.

- *<u>Evaluation Rubric:</u> Supporting Business Processes (sometimes called Secondary Business Processes) support the Operational Business Processes. They are the "back office" functions which do not usually have direct contact with customers. Examples of Supporting Business Processes in healthcare organizations - and in all organizations - are those related to human resources, facilities, and financial management. There is no right or wrong answer to this question. It just has to be reasoned and make sense.*

<u>Suggested Memo Content Item 6:</u> A brief description of how the Operational Business Processes and Supporting Business Processes are managed to ensure that they are functioning well and meeting the Use Case.

- Example: CHGH monitors the Operational Business Processes through patient surveys regarding whether they feel confident in the health care they receive from CHGH; that is, whether they have full confidence in the CHGH health care delivery personnel. Patients are also surveyed regarding whether they feel respected and treated as individuals as well as whether patients feel the facilities are clean and comfortable. If more than five percent of the survey respondents are dissatisfied with any of the items, then a review of the processes involved is undertaken. The review includes a review of human resources processes and facilities processes.

- *Evaluation Rubric: There is no right or wrong answer to this question. It just has to be reasoned and make sense.*

Suggested Memo Content Item 7: A brief description of the business processes used in your healthcare organization to stay current with innovations relevant to your healthcare organization. Also briefly state which innovation area is the one in which you expect to see the most innovation in the next five to ten years.

- Example: CHGH provides financial support to employees to attend conferences, vendor demonstrations, and networking events in innovation topic areas relevant to their workplace focus. Every six months CHGH asks for input from all employees regarding innovations not currently used by CHGH, but which should be used by CHGH. This input is organized by our CHGH Office of Innovation and distributed in a newsletter to all employees. The material in this newsletter is also discussed at a biannual meeting of all department chairs where decisions are made regarding which innovations to implement at CHGH. CHGH expects the most activity innovation to be in the area of Product/Technology Innovation.

- *Evaluation Rubric: There are three broad innovation areas: 1) Product/Technology Innovation – bringing a new product/technology or an existing product with new technology to market (produced at scale at a reasonable cost which meets a consumer need); 2) Process Innovation – a new method/process for producing products at scale and at a reasonable cost; 3) Business Model Innovation - a new method (a new business model) for selling a product to consumers. There is no right or wrong answer to this question. It just has to be reasoned and make sense.*

Suggested Memo Content Item 8: A brief description of your healthcare organization's relationship to entrepreneurship. That is, does your organization actively seek to generate spin-off companies? Why or why not? If yes, are there organizational business processes to support it?

- Example: CHGH encourages all employees to have an entrepreneurial attitude. All employees are encouraged to take their innovation ideas and work to the CHGH Office of Innovation. Personnel from the Office of Innovation also try and maintain routine contact with all CHGH employees to encourage entrepreneurship and innovation. The Office of Innovation has business processes in place to try and turn CHGH employee innovation ideas into spin-off companies

- *Evaluation Rubric: There is no right or wrong answer to this question. It just has to be reasoned and make sense.*

Suggested Memo Content Item 9: A brief description of the business processes used in your healthcare organization regarding electronic patient/customer records? For example, describe the extent to which your healthcare organization uses such software and for what purposes. If electronic patient/customer records are not used, why not? If electronic patient/customer records are used, are they Electronic Health Record (EHR) compatible? What is the relationship between your records and a patient's/customer's Personal Health Record (PHR)?

- Example: CHGH attempts to always use the most innovative Electronic Medical Record (EMR) available in the most cost-effective way. The CHGH Office of Technology is responsible for ensuring that the EMR functions well on a day-to-day basis as well as being the most up-to-date and in compliance with all mandated and recommended capabilities. The chosen EMR is EHR compliant. Patients/customers are able to access and download all EMR data to their PHR except the private clinical notes of health care delivery professionals.

Patients/customers are also encouraged to upload any PHR data they wish exchange/share with CHGH

- *Evaluation Rubric: There is no right or wrong answer to this question. It just has to be reasoned and make sense.*

*****

> *Video* [bib#556]: *The video for Topic 1 – **LibreOffice-Writer (1) A First Look** – is a YouTube video produced by TheFrugalComputerGuy. The video provides a brief introduction to the LibreOffice Writer word processing software. The link for the video is:*
> (https://www.youtube.com/watch?v=mc845_FuONY

*****

L4 Topic 2 (T2). Suggested format for the memo

The memo project suggests that you to synthesize course material to design patient-centered business processes in a healthcare organization the way you would have things run in the best of all worlds. The required synthesis items were described in Topic 1 of Lesson Four.

It is suggested that your synthesized information be presented (formatted/designed) as a memo developed using word processing software (e.g., Microsoft Word). There are many software options. Some are available at no cost such as Writer [bib#211] which is part of LibreOffice [bib#212]. An example of a completed memo project is found in *Appendix B: Memo Example*.

The electronic memo file is an artifact of the course which you can circulate to colleagues or use for a talk or presentation event. In constructing your memo, you are going to do so from the perspective of the chief healthcare administrator for your organization. You are describing your patient-centered health care delivery system to an audience.

The basic process for generating an effective electronic memo file is:

1. Choose the word processing software to use
2. Add the content
3. Iterate to improve

In the ***Lesson Four Self-Evaluations*** section of this book is a quiz entitled ***Generate an Effective Memo Self-Evaluation***. This quiz is a self-evaluation as to whether you have generated an effective electronic memo. It is a seven (7) question quiz asking whether you have incorporated the seven suggested format/design characteristics into your memo. These seven are only suggestions. The memo format/design is yours to choose. The seven suggested characteristics are:

Suggested Memo Format/Design Characteristic 1: The electronic memo is between 1 and 3 pages.

Suggested Memo Format/Design Characteristic 2: There is a page number on each page of the memo.

Suggested Memo Format/Design Characteristic 3: There is an adequate margin on each side of the page (one inch margin on top, bottom, left and right is recommended) .

Suggested Memo Format/Design Characteristic 4: One font-type is used for the entire memo. The chosen font-type is easily readable and not distracting from the content.

Suggested Memo Format/Design Characteristic 5: The font-size for the different content sections/types of the memo can be different, but the font-size is the same for each type of content section.

Suggested Memo Format/Design Characteristic 6: There is a title for the memo at the top of the first page which is less than 15 words and provides the reader with a clear understanding of the memo's focus.

Suggested Memo Format/Design Characteristic 7: The author of the memo is stated on the first page.

*****

> **Video** [bib#557]: *The first video for Topic 2 – **How to Write a Perfect Memo** – is a YouTube video produced by David Taylor. The video provides information on how to write the perfect memo. The link for the video is:*
> (https://www.youtube.com/watch?v=G_jErsVxjpM

*****

Some people feel cautious about writing memos because they feel unsure of the correct punctuation or grammar to use. However, there are many wonderful resources on these topics. One of the best is the Purdue Online Writing Lab (OWL) [bib#558].

*****

> **Video** [bib#559]: *The video for Topic 3 – **Purdue OWL: Visual Rhetoric** – is a YouTube video produced by Purdue Owl. It is an overview of visual rhetoric and when and how to use it. The link for the video is:*
> https://www.youtube.com/watch?v=-vJvivIzkDg

*****

L4 Self-Evaluations

At this point, you should have *Designed Healthcare Organization Business Processes* – if you have chosen to do so – within a healthcare organization the way you would have things run in the best of all worlds. The type of healthcare organization is your choice (e.g., physical therapy office, dentist office, pharmacy, hospital, doctor's office).

It is suggested that this design be organized as an electronic memo file according to the sixteen (16) items/criteria suggested earlier. As such, the last two (and in some ways the most important) competency development tasks are your personal evaluation of the electronic memo you developed.

The quality of a memo for presentation is usually judged on two major factors: 1) whether the memo content is sufficient for its intended purpose, and 2) whether the memo appearance is such that the content can be grasped relatively easily. Most memos are produced for a specific purpose (e.g., a conference, a meeting, an analysis) and the sufficiency of the content is related to its purpose. The quality of a memo for presentation (content presentation and format) is usually evaluated relative to its intended purpose.

For the purposes of this suggested competency development task, the evaluation criteria are the sixteen (16) suggested items/criteria discussed earlier. Clearly, you can ignore them and establish your own different criteria. An example of a completed memo with the sixteen (16) suggested items/criteria items – nine (9) suggested content items and the seven (7) suggested template/design characteristics – is found in *Appendix B: Memo Example*.

Your personal evaluation of your electronic memo – for the purposes of this suggested competency development task – is divided into two self-evaluations:

- Synthesize Content Self-Evaluation
- Generate an Effective Electronic Memo Self-Evaluation

The questions for each of the two self-evaluations are shown below.

L4 Quiz: Synthesize Content Self-Evaluation

Question 1

Does the memo display a name for the healthcare organization in which the patient-centered business processes are designed that is original and gives some sense to healthcare consumers as to the healthcare products found in the organization?

O   Yes

O   No

This is your own personal self-evaluation of the synthesized material suggested for the memo.

Question 2

Does the memo display a brief description of the healthcare organization (a description of what the healthcare organization does) which concisely and clearly summarizes for healthcare consumers the type of healthcare organization, its location, and its products in a few sentences?

O   Yes

O   No

This is your own personal self-evaluation of the synthesized material suggested for the memo.

Question 3

Does the memo display a brief, broad overview of the most important Use Case for the patient-centered healthcare organization; that is, the most important requirements patients have for your healthcare organization? There is no right or wrong answer to this question. It just has to be reasoned and make sense.

O   Yes

O   No

This is your own personal self-evaluation of the synthesized material suggested for the memo.

Question 4

Does the memo display a brief, broad overview of the Operational Business Processes most important to the Use Case? There is no right or wrong answer to this question. It just has to be reasoned and make sense.

O   Yes

O   No

This is your own personal self-evaluation of the synthesized material suggested for the memo.

Question 5

Does the memo display a brief, broad overview of the Supporting Business Processes most important to the Use Case? There is no right or wrong answer to this question. It just has to be reasoned and make sense.

O   Yes

O   No

This is your own personal self-evaluation of the synthesized material suggested for the memo.

Question 6

Does the memo display a brief description of how the Operational Business Processes and Supporting Business Processes are managed to ensure that they are functioning well and meeting the Use Case? There is no right or wrong answer to this question. It just has to be reasoned and make sense.

O   Yes

O   No

This is your own personal self-evaluation of the synthesized material suggested for the memo.

Question 7

Does the memo display a brief description of the business processes used in the healthcare organization to stay current with innovations relevant to the healthcare organization? Does the memo briefly state which innovation area is the one in which the memo author expects to see the most innovation in the next five to ten years? There is no right or wrong answer to this question. It just has to be reasoned and make sense.

O Yes

O No

This is your own personal self-evaluation of the synthesized material suggested for the memo.

Question 8

Does the memo displaya brief description of the healthcare organization's relationship to entrepreneurship? That is, does the memo describe whether the organization actively seeks to generate spin-off companies? Why or why not? If yes, are there organizational business processes to support it? There is no right or wrong answer to this question. It just has to be reasoned and make sense.

O Yes

O No

This is your own personal self-evaluation of the synthesized material suggested for the memo.

Question 9

Does the memo display a brief description of the business processes used in the healthcare organization regarding electronic patient/customer records? For example, does the memo describe the extent to which the healthcare organization uses such software and for what purposes? If electronic patient/customer records are not used, why not? If electronic patient/customer records are used, are they Electronic Health Record (EHR) compatible? What is the relationship between your records and a patient's/customer's Personal Health Record (PHR)? There is no right or wrong answer to this question. It just has to be reasoned and make sense.

O Yes

O No

This is your own personal self-evaluation of the synthesized material suggested for the memo.

L4 Quiz: Generate an Effective Electronic Memo Self-Evaluation

<u>Question 1</u>

Is your electronic memo is between 1 and 3 pages?

O   Yes
O   No

This is your own personal self-evaluation of the format/design suggested for the memo.

<u>Question 2</u>

Is there is a page number on each page of your memo?

O   Yes
O   No

This is your own personal self-evaluation of the format/design suggested for the memo.

<u>Question 3</u>

Is there an adequate margin on each side of the page (one inch margin on top, bottom, left and right is recommended)?

O   Yes
O   No

This is your own personal self-evaluation of the format/design suggested for the memo.

<u>Question 4</u>

Is one font-type is used for your entire memo? Is the chosen font-type is easily readable and not distracting from the content?

O   Yes
O   No

This is your own personal self-evaluation of the format/design suggested for the memo.

Question 5

Is the font-size the same for each type of content section? It can be different for the different content sections/types of the memo.

O   Yes
O   No

This is your own personal self-evaluation of the format/design suggested for the memo.

Question 6

Is there is a title for your memo at the top of the first page which is less than 15 words and provides the reader with a clear understanding of the memo's focus?

O   Yes
O   No

This is your own personal self-evaluation of the format/design suggested for the memo.

Question 7

Is the name of the memo's author stated on the first page?

O   Yes
O   No

This is your own personal self-evaluation of the format/design suggested for the memo.

L4 Discussion Question: Memo Generation

What, if anything, surprised you most about the process of producing an electronic memo? What, if anything, surprised you most about the process of judging a memo? What did you find most interesting, challenging, fun, ...?

L4 Trivia Question and Virtual Field Trip

L4 Trivia Question

Almost everyone loves a trivia question – a question about a little known, but interesting, fun fact. Each lesson has one trivia question. The answer is in the Lesson Four Trivia Question Answer reading section.

Question:

Coin clipping is the act of illegally shaving off a small amount of a coin made from a precious metal (e.g., silver) to obtain and sell the metal. In the late 1600s in England, coin clipping was a serious problem. The coins became smaller and irregularly shaped as a result of the coin clipping which made them unusable as currency. A financial crisis loomed until the Warden at the Royal Mint devised a solution to stop coin clipping. *Who was the Warden and what was the solution?*

L4 Trivia Question Answer

The answer to the Lesson Four trivia question is:

The Warden was Issac Newton and the solution was ridges along the edges of coins

For more information, please see:

- How Isaac Newton helped shape our coins [bib#560]

- [Top 10 Isaac Newton Inventions: The Perfect Coin](#) [bib#561]
- [Methods of coin debasement, Wikipedia](#) [bib#562]
- [The Royal Mint Museum, Issac Newton](#) [bib#563]

L4 Virtual Field Trip

Everyone loves a road trip/field trip so each lesson of the course includes a "*virtual field trip*" to the often hidden places of interest on the web.

Lesson Four's virtual field trip is to the [Frick Collection](#) [bib#564] in New York City which is:

"*Internationally recognized as a premier museum and research center, the Frick is known for its distinguished Old Master paintings and outstanding examples of European sculpture and decorative arts. The collection was assembled by the Pittsburgh industrialist Henry Clay Frick (1849–1919) and is housed in his former residence on Fifth Avenue. One of New York City's few remaining Gilded Age mansions, it provides a tranquil environment for visitors to experience masterpieces by artists such as Bellini, Rembrandt, Vermeer, Gainsborough, Goya, and Whistler. The museum opened in 1935 and has continued to acquire works of art since Mr. Frick's death.*"

Henry Clay Frick became partners with [Andrew Carnegie](#) [bib#565] in 1882. Although friendly for most of their partnership, they had a serious falling out. It is reported that toward the end of both their lives, Carnegie sent word to Frick that he wished to meet with Frick to make amends. Frick would have none of it. [Frick is reported to have responded](#) [bib#566] to Carnegie's messenger: "*Yes, you can tell Carnegie I'll meet him. Tell him I'll see him in Hell, where we both are going.*"

More information about Henry Clay Frick can be found at:

- [Henry Clay Frick](#) [bib#567]
- [Henry Clay Frick, Wikipedia](#) [bib#568]

- [Henry Clay Frick (1849-1919)](#) [bib#569]
- [Frick, Henry Clay](#) [bib#570]

*****

> ***Video*** [bib#571]: *The video for the Lesson Four Virtual Field Trip –* **Introduction to The Frick Collection** *– is a YouTube video produced by the Frick Collection. The video is an overview and a tour of the Frick Collection in New York City. The link for the video is:*
> https://www.youtube.com/watch?v=LEyC8g94MZE

*****

L4 Wrapping Up

Book content included an overview of healthcare organization business processes including business process management approaches as well as a discussion of healthcare organization entrepreneurship as a business process. If you have completed all of the competency development tasks you should have a better understanding of business processes and entrepreneurship in healthcare organizations. If you work within a healthcare organization you should now be better able to contribute to the efficient and effective operations of your organization. You should be better able to undertake and improve healthcare business process management system responsibilities within your organization.

The overall competency goal of this book was that it enabled you to think more critically and more independently about business processes in healthcare organizations.

Specifically, upon successful completion of this book, you should now be able to:

1. Define healthcare organization business processes and business process management.

2. Define healthcare organization business process management improvement and innovation.

3. Define healthcare organization electronic patient/customer records business processes.

4. Synthesize course content to create patient-centered business processes for a healthcare organization.

5. Generate an effective memo suitable for discussion, presentation, and printing.

The hope embedded in this book is that having achieved these objectives, you do not just know more now that you have read this book, but that you now think more critically and more independently about healthcare organization business processes and entrepreneurship.

If a personal goal is to be the best healthcare administrator: Find excellent mentors in healthcare administration. Find excellent healthcare administration peers. Do more healthcare administration than anyone else (e.g., read more about healthcare administration than anyone else, do more healthcare administration tasks than anyone else). It is hoped that the extra resources in this book (e.g., external links) help you accomplish these three steps.

But wherever your learning path and journey take you, the hope embedded in this book is that your path and journey are as pleasant and interesting as many of those which can be found in the National Parks of the United States [bib#572]. Some truly spectacular paths can be found in Glacier National Park [bib#573] in Montana.

*****

> **Video** [bib#574]: *The video for this Wrapping Up section –*
> ***Scenic Hikes in Eastern Glacier National Park*** *– is a*
> *YouTube video produced by Amazing Places on Our Planet.*
> *The video is an overview of three hikes in Glacier National*
> *Park.. The link for the video i*s:
> https://www.youtube.com/watch?v=BxikeSMhXXY

*****

L4 Discussion Question: Achievement of Personal Learning Goal

At the beginning of this book, you were asked to consider whether you had a personal learning goal for this learning path. If you did, was your goal achieved? Did you learn what you wanted to learn in this book? If not, what resources do you need to achieve your personal learning goal? What are your next steps?

Appendix A: Expanded Book Overview

The *About this Book* section at the beginning of this book gives a very brief overview of the book content and intent.   A longer, expanded overview is provided in this section. Appendix A is redundant with the information contained in the *About this Book* section. Appendix A is provided because some readers prefer a more detailed overview of the book than is provided in the *About this Book* section. This longer overview addresses five (5) topics organized as questions with answers. The questions/topics are:

1. What is a brief summary of this book?
2. How is the book content organized?
3. What are the competency objectives for readers?
4. What tasks facilitate development of competency objectives?
5. What is the educational philosophy of this book?

Appendix A Topic 1. What is a brief summary of this book?

Have you ever needed to resolve a billing or scheduling issue with a healthcare organization and thought that there must be a better, more efficient, and more customer-friendly way to operate such a business process? For example, have you found yourself thinking that there should be an easier way to read your bill or pay or bill? Or do you work in a healthcare organization and find yourself thinking that there must be better ways for the business processes to function? If you have, this course is for you.

This book is for you if you are interested in the world of business processes and business process management in healthcare organizations in the United States. The book is suitable for those with a developing interest in healthcare organization operations as they pertain to business processes and their management. It is also suitable for those who have some expertise, but who wish an overview or refresher of these topics.

This book is for those with a developing interest in the organizational operations, administration, and business process improvement in healthcare organizations and for those who have some expertise, but who wish an overview or refresher of these topics.

This book has an agenda or purpose aimed at aiding the reader. The book knows that you have your own specific personal goals regarding business process improvement in healthcare. The purpose of this book is to enable you to develop your own learning path to reach your learning goal regardless of what that goal happens to be. The intent of the book is to provide you with content and resources to pursue a personal learning path. That content extends past the reading of this text and will help you in your chosen work or study.

The format includes tons of resources (some would say encyclopedic) coupled with the Socratic Method and suggested competency development tasks. The Socratic Method promotes understanding of a topic by posing questions on that topic. An answer to the question requires a learner/reader to think critically and synthesize information. The overall competency goal for all readers of this book is that it enables each reader to think more critically and more independently about business process improvement in healthcare organizations.

The book is organized into four (4) lessons. Each lesson is organized around competency objectives, questions, readings, competency development tasks (e.g., quiz) to organize your thinking and cement your learning. It is a format which makes extensive use of the resources available on the internet. As such the book provides links to external sites to connect you to the larger "*real world*" of healthcare organizations to help you better build your own learning path. The links also serve as resources you can use after you complete this book. We want to emphasize that the list of resources provided for the reader is an important and valuable aspect of this book.

These links (more than 550) are directly accessible in the content in the e-book version. For the print version – and for reference in the e-book version – the full URL for each link in the book can be found at the corresponding in-text link number [bib#] in the section at the end of the book entitled *Bibliography: Associated URL/Link List*. The list includes data, management, and research links needed for healthcare administration, management, and operations related to business processes in a healthcare organization.

The competency development tasks in this book facilitate content mastery to help you organize your thinking. Such organized thought should help you determine the relationship between the book content, a personal learning path, and achievement of personal goals. Competency development tasks in this book are: discussion questions, quizzes, and a project. Again, this is a Socratic approach in that the book asks for your thinking on the topics.

The included suggested project is intended to help you synthesize content material by developing business processes for a healthcare organization of your choice the way you would have things run in the best of all worlds. The suggested design format to communicate these business processes is an electronic memo format. An example of a completed memo project is found in *Appendix B: Memo Example*. The memo is an artifact which you can circulate to colleagues or use as the basis for a talk or presentation event. The philosophy behind this project is that more learning occurs – and learning is more fun – if you can actually build/create something from the content and it is useful beyond the reading of this book.

And because everyone loves a road trip/field trip, there are also "*virtual field trips*" to the often hidden places of interest on the web. There are also trivia questions – just for fun – because everyone also loves little known, but interesting, fun facts.

This book is dense in the physics sense of the word. There is a lot of detail we have to introduce to get people on the playing field. There is no royal road to acquiring that depth of information. We have attempted to organize the information and to make it searchable. One needs to take a break every so often to absorb the material. This is one of the reasons why virtual field trips and trivia questions are provided. Historical and social context is important in healthcare. Many of the links, virtual field trips, and trivia questions provide this context.

This book follows the content of and can be used as an adjunct to the Coursera course: *Business Process Management in Healthcare Organizations* found at https://www.coursera.org/learn/business-process-management-in-healthcare-organizations. Should you prefer a learning experience which can result in an earned certificate or prefer a community of learners in the same course of study, consider enrolling in the Coursera course.

Appendix A Topic 2. How is the book content organized?

The book is organized into four (4) lessons. Each lesson should take 4 - 6 hours of work to successfully complete; total time commitment for the course of study defined by the book = 16 - 24 hours. The four lessons are:

1. Healthcare Organization Business Processes and Management *(Primary Competency Development Task: Quiz)*

2. Healthcare Organization Business Process Management Improvement and Innovation *(Primary Competency Development Task: Quiz)*

3. Healthcare Organization Electronic Patient/Customer Records Business Processes Organizations *(Primary Competency Development Task: Quiz)*

4. Design Patient-Centered Healthcare Organization Business Processes *(Primary Competency Development Task: Business Process Management Memo Project)*

It is suggested that your synthesized information be presented (formatted/designed) as a memo developed using word processing software (e.g., Microsoft Word). An example of a completed memo project is found in *Appendix B: Memo Example*. The memo is an artifact of the book which you can circulate to colleagues or use for a talk or presentation event. For the suggested memo project, you will need word processing software. There are many software options. Some are available at no cost such as Writer [bib#211] which is part of LibreOffice [bib#212].

Each lesson is organized around readings, videos, and competency development tasks (i.e., discussion question, quiz, project) to organize your thinking and cement your learning with regard to the stated competency objective(s) for that lesson. The competency development tasks in this book facilitate content mastery to help you organize your thinking. Such organized thought should help you determine the relationship between the book content, a personal learning path, and achievement of personal goals. Again, this is a Socratic approach in that the book asks for your thinking on the topics.

- Again, readings are presented as a series of topic questions and answers – the Socratic Method – because it is a better and much more interesting way for a reader to master content.

- Some of the links in the book are to YouTube videos. Most of these videos are used to present interesting supplemental content to the readings and are not needed to complete the competency development tasks. Some link to a "*virtual field trip*" to the often hidden places of interest on the web.

- Each discussion question is a competency development task intended to help you consider important and interesting questions related to the readings content. The question is suitable for either discussion with others or your own personal thought and reflection. The purpose of the question is to facilitate critical, independent – as well as possibly new and interesting – ways to think about health care delivery in healthcare organizations.

- There are two types of quizzes in this book: content and self-evaluation. Each type of quiz is a competency development task. The first type contains multiple choice or fill-in-the-blank questions based in the designated readings. The purpose of each content quiz is to help you develop competency in the stated study objectives. There is nothing like being asked a question about a topic to help you learn and think critically about that topic. The answer key for each content quiz is at the end of the content quiz. The second type is a self-evaluation of the memo project content and format to ensure that you think critically about the memo project (e.g., if the reflects a synthesis of content), if you have chosen to develop a memo.

- The included memo project is a competency development task intended to help you synthesize content material by designing healthcare organization business processes of your choice the way you would have things run in the best of all worlds. The design is communicated in a memo format. The memo project is an artifact which you can circulate to colleagues or use as the basis for a talk or presentation event. The philosophy behind this project is that more learning occurs – and learning is more fun – if you can actually build/create something from the content (rather than just being tested on the content) and is useful beyond the reading of this book. There is nothing like being asked to create and present content on a topic to help you learn and think critically about that topic. An example of a completed memo project is found in *Appendix B: Memo Example*.

- There are also trivia questions – just for fun – because everyone also loves little known, but interesting, fun facts.

Appendix A Topic 3. What are the competency objectives for readers?

The overall competency goal of this book is that **it** enables you to think more critically and more independently about business processes in healthcare organizations in new and interesting ways.

Specifically, upon successful completion of this book (e.g., the readings, the suggested competency development tasks), you should be able to:

1. Define healthcare organization business processes and business process management.

2. Define healthcare organization business process management improvement and innovation.

3. Define healthcare organization electronic patient/customer records business processes.

4. Synthesize course content to create patient-centered business processes for a healthcare organization.

5. Generate an effective memo suitable for discussion, presentation, and printing.

The hope embedded in this book is that having achieved these objectives, you do not just know more now that you have read this book, but that you now think more critically and more independently about healthcare organization business processes in new and interesting ways.

As a result of achieving the competency objectives you should have a better understanding of healthcare organizations and their business processes. Readers working within a healthcare organization should be better able to contribute to the efficient and effective operations of their organization as a whole as well as the organization's business process management and entrepreneurship. They will be able to undertake and improve healthcare administration and management responsibilities within their organization.

Appendix A Topic 4. What tasks facilitate achievement of competency objectives?

Competency development tasks include discussion questions, quizzes, and a memo project. The competency development tasks in this book facilitate content mastery to help you organize your thinking.

Competency development tasks include discussion questions, quizzes, and a memo project. The competency development tasks in this book facilitate content mastery to help you organize your thinking.

Appendix A Task: Discussion Question

Each discussion question is a competency development task intended to help you consider important and interesting questions related to the readings content. The question is suitable for either discussion with others or your own personal thought and reflection. The purpose of the question is to facilitate critical, independent – as well as possibly new and interesting – ways to think about healthcare organization business processes. Each lesson includes at least one discussion question. The discussion questions in this book address the following topics:

- Personal Learning Goal for this Learning Path (Lesson One)

- External/Environmental Challenges for Healthcare Organizations (Lesson One)

- Disruptive Innovation in Healthcare (Lesson Two)

- Exchange and Use of Your Personal Health Data (Lesson Three)

- Memo Generation (Lesson Four)

- Achievement of Personal Learning Goal (Lesson Four)

Appendix A Task: Quiz

There are two types of quizzes in this book: content and self-evaluation. Each type of quiz is a competency development task. The first type contains multiple choice or fill-in-the-blank questions based in the designated readings. The purpose of each content quiz is to help you develop competency in the stated study objectives. There is nothing like being asked a question about a topic to help you learn and think critically about that topic. The answer key for each content quiz is at the end of the content quiz. The three content quizzes are:

- Lesson One Quiz
- Lesson Two Quiz
- Lesson Three Quiz

The second type of quiz is a self-evaluation of the memo project content and format to ensure that you think critically about the memo (e.g., if the reflects a synthesis of content), if you have chosen to develop a memo. The two self-evaluation quizzes are:

- Synthesize Content Self-Evaluation (Lesson Four)
- Generate an Effective Memo Self-Evaluation (Lesson Four)

Appendix A Task: Memo Project

The included memo project is a competency development task intended to help you synthesize content material by designing a healthcare organization business process management system of your choice the way you would have things run in the best of all worlds. The design is communicated in a memo format. The content for the memo t is your design for a business process management system. As such, there are no right or wrong content items. There are only sensible and reasonable items within the content criteria specified in the book. There is also no one right way to organize the memo format. There are only sensible and reasonable format aspects within the criteria specified in the course of study. Once you have produced the memo, you should evaluate your memo using the two self-evaluation quizzes.

The memo is an artifact which you can circulate to colleagues or use as the basis for a talk or presentation event.   The philosophy behind this project is that more learning occurs – and learning is more fun – if you can actually build/create something from the content (rather than just being tested on the content) and is useful beyond the reading of this book.   There is nothing like being asked to create and present content on a topic to help you learn and think critically about that topic An example of a completed memo project is found in *Appendix B: Memo Example*.

Appendix A Topic 5. What is the educational philosophy of this book?

The educational philosophy of this book, unlike most other texts, is based in an agenda or purpose aimed at aiding the reader. The book assumes that all readers have their own specific personal goals regarding health care delivery systems in healthcare organizations (e.g., improve health care delivery system skills, improve healthcare administration skills, learn more about healthcare organizations in general). It also assumes that readers have different specific goals.

The primary educational philosophy of the book is, therefore, that readers should be provided with enough content and resources to pursue a personally chosen learning path. Readers should be able to choose a personally customized learning path within the book content which leads to the achievement of personal goals. The provided content should encourage reader independence and critical thinking. Content should extend past the reading of this text and help readers in their chosen work or study. The content of the book should connect readers to the larger world and resources available on the internet.

As such the book provides links to external sites to connect readers to the larger "*real world*" of healthcare organizations to help readers better build their own personal, customized learning path. These links (more than 575) are directly accessible in the content in the e-book version. For the print version – and for reference in the e-book version – the full URL for each link in the book can be found at the corresponding in-text link number *(bib#)* in the section at the end of the book entitled *Bibliography: Associated URL/Link List*. The links also serve as resources which can be used after the book is completed. The list includes data, management, and research links needed for healthcare administration, management, and operations.

Another major philosophical approach of the book is use of the Socratic Method and learning by doing. The Socratic Method promotes understanding of a topic by posing questions on that topic. An answer to the question requires a learner/reader to think critically and synthesize information. Again, reading content is presented as a series of topic questions and answers – the Socratic

Method – because it is a better and much more interesting way for a reader to master content. The project requires readers to synthesize course material to design a healthcare organization and governance structure the way the reader would have things run in the best of all worlds. The philosophy behind this project is that more learning occurs – and learning is more fun – if a reader can actually build/create something from the course of study content (rather than just being tested on the content) and show this built/created artifact to others (learning by doing).

Appendix B: Memo Example

The following few pages contain an example of a completed memo which has the required format/design characteristics and the required content.

MEMO

Subject: Overview of the Patient-Centered Business Processes at Charles Harbor General Hospital (CHGH)
To: Community of Those Interested in CHGH
From: I.M. Incharge, CEO

CHGH Description: Charles Harbor General Hospital (CHGH) is a private, non-profit, general hospital in Massachusetts. It has an emergency room and a full range of clinical specialties (e.g., internal medicine, general surgery, oncology, cardiology, infectious disease, pediatrics).

Most Important Patient-Centered Business Process Use Case: CHGH patients want to feel confident in the health care they receive from CHGH; that is, patients want to have full confidence in the CHGH health care delivery personnel. Patients also want to feel respected and treated as individuals. Patients also want the facilities to be clean and comfortable.

Operational Business Processes Most Important to the Use Case: For the CHGH Use Case requirements to be met, CHGH must have superior, patient-centered health care delivery personnel and excellent health care delivery facilities and equipment.

Supporting Business Processes Most Important to the Use Case: For the CHGH Use Case requirements to be met, CHGH must have superior human resources personnel and processes to ensure that the health care delivery personnel are superior and patient-centered. CHGH also needs superior facilities personnel and processes to ensure that health care delivery facilities and equipment are superior, clean, and comfortable.

Management of Operational Business Processes and Supporting Business Processes to Ensure They Are Functioning Well and Meeting the Use Case: CHGH monitors the Operational Business Processes through patient surveys regarding whether they feel confident in the health care they receive from CHGH; that is, whether they have full confidence in the CHGH health care delivery personnel. Patients are also surveyed regarding whether they feel respected and treated as individuals as well as whether patients feel the facilities are clean and comfortable. If more than five percent of the survey respondents are dissatisfied with any of the items, then a review of the processes involved is undertaken. The review includes a review of human resources processes and facilities processes.

Business Processes Used to Stay Current with Innovations Relevant to CHGH: CHGH provides financial support to employees to attend conferences, vendor demonstrations, and networking events in innovation topic areas relevant to their workplace focus. Every six months CHGH asks for input from all employees regarding innovations not currently used by CHGH, but which should be used by CHGH. This input is organized by our CHGH Office of Innovation and distributed in a newsletter to all employees. The material in this newsletter is also discussed at a biannual meeting of all department chairs where decisions are made regarding which innovations to implement at CHGH. CHGH expects the most innovation to be in the area of Product/Technology Innovation.

Entrepreneurship Business Processes: CHGH encourages all employees to have an entrepreneurial attitude. All employees are encouraged to take their innovation ideas and work to the CHGH Office of Innovation. Personnel from the Office of Innovation also try and maintain routine contact with all CHGH employees to encourage entrepreneurship and innovation. The Office of Innovation has business processes in place to try and turn CHGH employee innovation ideas into spin-off companies.

Electronic Patient/Customer Records Business Processes: CHGH attempts to always use the most innovative Electronic Medical Record (EMR) available in the most cost-effective way. The CHGH Office of Technology is responsible for ensuring that the EMR functions well on a day-to-day basis as well as being the most up-to-date and in compliance with all mandated and recommended capabilities. The chosen EMR is Electronic Health Record (EHR) compliant. Patients/customers are able to access and download all EMR data to their Personal Health Record (PHR) except the private clinical notes of health care delivery professionals. Patients/customers are also encouraged to upload any PHR data they wish to exchange/share with CHGH

Bibliography: Associated URL/Link List

1. Book Text: *Fisher Fine Arts Library, University of Pennsylvania* Link Associated with Text: https://www.library.upenn.edu/finearts
2. Book Text: *Image from Wikipedia, File:Furness Lib interior looking N UPenn.JPG* Link Associated with Text: https://en.wikipedia.org/wiki/File:Furness_Lib_interior_looking_N_UPenn.JPG
3. Book Text: *Suzzallo Library, University of Washington* Link Associated with Text: https://www.lib.washington.edu/suzzallo/visit/about
4. Book Text: *Image from Wikipedia, File:MK03235 University of Washington Suzzallo Library.jpg* Link Associated with Text: https://en.wikipedia.org/wiki/File:MK03235_University_of_Washington_Suzzallo_Library.jpg
5. Book Text: *William W. Cook Legal Research Library, University of Michigan* Link Associated with Text: http://www.law.umich.edu/historyandtraditions/buildings/LegalResearchLibrary/Pages/default.aspx
6. Book Text: *Image from Wikipedia, File:UniversityofMichiganLawLibrary.jpg* Link Associated with Text: https://en.wikipedia.org/wiki/File:UniversityofMichiganLawLibrary.jpg
7. Book Text: *Video: Kenn Borek Air's South Pole Rescue Team - 2017 National Air and Space Museum Trophy Winner* Link Associated with Text: https://www.youtube.com/watch?v=XGc-o1ufjjY
8. Book Text: *Business Dictionary* Link Associated with Text: http://www.businessdictionary.com/definition/business-process.html
9. Book Text: *Business Process Management Glossary* Link Associated with Text: https://www.gluu.biz/process-management-glossary/business-process-definition
10. Book Text: *American College of Healthcare Executives (ACHE)* Link Associated with Text: https://www.ache.org/-/media/ache/fache/bogexamreferencemanual.pdf
11. Book Text: *Adam Smith* Link Associated with Text: https://en.wikipedia.org/wiki/Adam_Smith
12. Book Text: *Wealth of Nations* Link Associated with Text: https://www.adamsmith.org/the-wealth-of-nations/
13. Book Text: *Railway Time* Link Associated with Text: https://en.wikipedia.org/wiki/Railway_time
14. Book Text: *Standard Time* Link Associated with Text: https://en.wikipedia.org/wiki/Standard_time
15. Book Text: *Daylight Saving Time* Link Associated with Text: https://en.wikipedia.org/wiki/Daylight_saving_time

16. Book Text: *collided head-on* Link Associated with Text: http://www.gendisasters.com/rhode-island/7410/pawtucket-ri-terrible-railroad-accident-aug-1853

17. Book Text: *Greenwich Mean Time (GMT)* Link Associated with Text: https://en.wikipedia.org/wiki/Greenwich_Mean_Time

18. Book Text: *solar time* Link Associated with Text: https://en.wikipedia.org/wiki/Solar_time

19. Book Text: *local mean time* Link Associated with Text: https://en.wikipedia.org/wiki/Local_mean_time

20. Book Text: *Charles Dowd* Link Associated with Text: https://en.wikipedia.org/wiki/Charles_F._Dowd

21. Book Text: *William F. Allen's proposal* Link Associated with Text: http://allencbrowne.blogspot.com/2017/03/william-frederick-allen.html

22. Book Text: *implemented on November 18, 1883* Link Associated with Text: http://americanhistory.si.edu/ontime/synchronizing/zones.html

23. Book Text: *Standard Time Act of 1918* Link Associated with Text: https://en.wikipedia.org/wiki/Standard_Time_Act

24. Book Text: *has jurisdiction over* Link Associated with Text: https://en.wikipedia.org/wiki/History_of_time_in_the_United_States

25. Book Text: *The Uniform Time Act of 1966* Link Associated with Text: https://en.wikipedia.org/wiki/Uniform_Time_Act

26. Book Text: *Video: A Breathtaking 110-Mile Alaskan Railroad Built in Two Years* Link Associated with Text: https://www.youtube.com/watch?v=7_nJhW8tmws

27. Book Text: *White Pass & Yukon* Link Associated with Text: https://wpyr.com/

28. Book Text: *the checklist is not ordered in the most efficient workflow* Link Associated with Text: https://aviation.stackexchange.com/questions/12707/what-is-the-difference-between-a-flow-and-a-checklist

29. Book Text: *pre-flight checklist* Link Associated with Text: https://en.wikipedia.org/wiki/Preflight_checklist

30. Book Text: *October 30, 1935 crash* Link Associated with Text: https://www.thisdayinaviation.com/30-october-1935/

31. Book Text: *(WHO) Surgical Safety Checklist* Link Associated with Text: http://www.who.int/patientsafety/safesurgery/checklist/en/

32. Book Text: *Keystone ICU Project* Link Associated with Text: https://www.hopkinsmedicine.org/news/media/releases/safety_checklist_use_yields_10_percent_drop_in_hospital_deaths

33. Book Text: *Peter J. Pronovost* Link Associated with Text: https://en.wikipedia.org/wiki/Peter_Pronovost

34. Book Text: *catheter-related bloodstream infections* Link Associated with Text: https://www.nejm.org/doi/full/10.1056/NEJMoa061115

35. Book Text: *impact of the use of these two (and other) checklists* Link Associated with Text: https://www.nature.com/news/hospital-checklists-are-meant-to-save-lives-so-why-do-they-often-fail-1.18057

36. Book Text: *report vast improvements* Link Associated with Text: https://ergoweb.com/checklists-improving-outcomes-for-icu-and-surgical-patients/

37. Book Text: *Website Source of Quote1* Link Associated with Text: https://qualitysafety.bmj.com/content/24/7/428#ref-1

38. Book Text: *Website Source of Quote2* Link Associated with Text: https://psnet.ahrq.gov/primer/checklists

39. Book Text: *Use Case* Link Associated with Text: https://en.wikipedia.org/wiki/Use_case

40. Book Text: *usability.gov* Link Associated with Text: https://www.usability.gov/

41. Book Text: *website use case* Link Associated with Text: https://www.usability.gov/how-to-and-tools/methods/use-cases.html

42. Book Text: *commonly used definition* Link Associated with Text: https://social-biz.org/2014/01/27/one-common-definition-for-bpm/

43. Book Text: *defines BPM* Link Associated with Text: http://www.bpminstitute.org/resources/articles/what-bpm-anyway-business-process-management-explained

44. Book Text: *BPMInstitute* Link Associated with Text: http://www.bpminstitute.org/about

45. Book Text: *certificates* Link Associated with Text: http://www.bpminstitute.org/certificates

46. Book Text: *(BPMP) certificate* Link Associated with Text: http://www.bpminstitute.org/certificates/business-process-management

47. Book Text: *International defines BPM* Link Associated with Text: https://www.abpmp.org/page/BPM_Profession

48. Book Text: *ABPMP International* Link Associated with Text: https://www.abpmp.org/

49. Book Text: *number of certificates* Link Associated with Text: https://www.abpmp.org/page/certification_home

50. Book Text: *(CBPP) certificate* Link Associated with Text: https://www.abpmp.org/page/CBPP_App_Process

51. Book Text: *BPM.com* Link Associated with Text: https://bpm.com/

52. Book Text: *Workflow Management Coalition (WfMC)* Link Associated with Text: http://www.wfmc.org/

53. Book Text: *Project Management Docs, Business Process Document* Link Associated with Text: https://www.projectmanagementdocs.com/template/project-documents/business-process-document/#ixzz5S9EfYLIz

54. Book Text: *smartsheet, Free Process Document Templates* Link Associated with Text: https://www.smartsheet.com/free-process-document-templates

55. Book Text: *Intelivate, Process Documentation – Protecting the Lifeline of Your Business Operations (Includes Process Templates)* Link Associated with Text: https://www.intelivate.com/team-strategy/process-documentation-why-and-how

56. Book Text: *TEMPLATE.NET, 13+ Business Process Examples* Link Associated with Text: https://www.template.net/business/business-process-examples/

57. Book Text: *Creately Blog, What is Process Documentation - The Easy Guide to Process Documentation* Link Associated with Text: https://creately.com/blog/diagrams/process-documentation-guide/

58. Book Text: *40 Use Case Templates & Examples (Word, PDF)* Link Associated with Text: https://templatelab.com/use-case-templates/

59. Book Text: *BPMN* Link Associated with Text: https://en.wikipedia.org/wiki/Business_Process_Model_and_Notation

60. Book Text: *Object Management Group* Link Associated with Text: https://www.omg.org/

61. Book Text: *OMG-BPMN* Link Associated with Text: http://www.bpmn.org/

62. Book Text: *Microsoft Visio* Link Associated with Text: https://www.microsoft.com/en-us/microsoft-365/visio/flowchart-software

63. Book Text: *free alternatives to Visio* Link Associated with Text: https://twitgoo.com/best-visio-alternatives/

64. Book Text: *Lucidchart* Link Associated with Text: https://www.lucidchart.com/

65. Book Text: *Creately* Link Associated with Text: https://creately.com/

66. Book Text: *LibreOffice Draw* Link Associated with Text: https://www.libreoffice.org/discover/draw/

67. Book Text: *Video: How to Create Flowcharts Using LibreOffice Draw* Link Associated with Text: https://www.youtube.com/watch?v=JHnUZLyPoUw

68. Book Text: *Flowcharting Medical Processes - Research* Link Associated with Text: https://research.vuse.vanderbilt.edu/King/flowcharting_medical_processes.ppt

69. Book Text: *Edraw, Free Workflow Diagram Templates for Word, PowerPoint, PDF* Link Associated with Text: https://www.edrawsoft.com/workflowdiagramtemplate.php

70. Book Text: *TEMPLATE.NET, 20+ Workflow Diagram Templates – Sample, Example, Format Download* Link Associated with Text: https://www.template.net/design-templates/print/sample-workflow-diagram-template/

71. Book Text: *Lucidchart, Flowchart Examples and Templates* Link Associated with Text:
https://www.lucidchart.com/pages/templates/flowchart
72. Book Text: *Creately, Flowchart Templates & Examples - Download for Free* Link Associated with Text: https://creately.com/diagram-type/templates/flowcharts
73. Book Text: *All About Business Process Mapping, Flow Charts and Diagrams* Link Associated with Text:
https://www.lucidchart.com/pages/business-process-mapping
74. Book Text: *Step-By-Step Guide to Business Process Mapping* Link Associated with Text: https://tallyfy.com/business-process-mapping/
75. Book Text: *Smartdraw, Business Process Map* Link Associated with Text: https://www.smartdraw.com/business-process-mapping/
76. Book Text: *Essential Guide to Business Process Mapping* Link Associated with Text: https://www.smartsheet.com/essential-guide-business-process-mapping
77. Book Text: *use case diagram (UML use case diagram)* Link Associated with Text: https://whatis.techtarget.com/definition/use-case-diagram
78. Book Text: *Process Flowchart VS Use Case Diagram* Link Associated with Text:
https://www.edrawsoft.com/processvsusecase.php
79. Book Text: *BPMN Tutorial: Quick-Start Guide to Business Process Model and Notation* Link Associated with Text:
https://www.process.st/bpmn-tutorial/
80. Book Text: *BPMN & BPMN 2.0 Tutorial* Link Associated with Text:
https://www.lucidchart.com/pages/bpmn-bpmn-2.0-tutorial
81. Book Text: *Process mapping as a framework for performance improvement in emergency general surgery* Link Associated with Text: https://www.ncbi.nlm.nih.gov/pmc/articles/PMC5785284/
82. Book Text: *Creately, Patient Check in Process* Link Associated with Text:
https://creately.com/diagram/example/hd9hm2oo1/Patient%20Check%20in%20Process
83. Book Text: *Flowchart* Link Associated with Text:
https://healthit.ahrq.gov/health-it-tools-and-resources/evaluation-resources/workflow-assessment-health-it-toolkit/all-workflow-tools/flowchart
84. Book Text: *Patient Check-In Flowchart* Link Associated with Text:
https://healthit.ahrq.gov/sites/default/files/docs/workflowtoolkit/PatientCheckIn.pdf
85. Book Text: *Emergency Department Workflow Diagrams* Link Associated with Text:
https://www.ahrq.gov/sites/default/files/wysiwyg/professionals/quality-

patient-safety/quality-resources/tools/cap-toolkit/ed-workflowdiagrams.pdf

86. Book Text: *Primary Care Workflow Diagrams* Link Associated with Text: https://www.ahrq.gov/sites/default/files/wysiwyg/professionals/quality-patient-safety/quality-resources/tools/cap-toolkit/pc-workflowdiagrams.pdf

87. Book Text: *Common Office Visit Flowchart* Link Associated with Text: https://healthit.ahrq.gov/sites/default/files/docs/workflowtoolkit/CFF_Office_Visit.pdf

88. Book Text: *Nurse-Only Visit Flowchart* Link Associated with Text: https://healthit.ahrq.gov/sites/default/files/docs/workflowtoolkit/NurseOnlyVisit.pdf

89. Book Text: *Physician Assistant (PA) Office Visit Flowchart* Link Associated with Text: https://healthit.ahrq.gov/sites/default/files/docs/workflowtoolkit/PAOfficeVisit.pdf

90. Book Text: *Medicine Today, Clinical Flowcharts* Link Associated with Text: https://medicinetoday.com.au/clinical-flowcharts

91. Book Text: *In-Office Prescribing Flowchart - Paper System* Link Associated with Text: https://healthit.ahrq.gov/sites/default/files/docs/workflowtoolkit/In-officePrescribing-PaperSystem.pdf

92. Book Text: *50 million inpatient surgical procedures* Link Associated with Text: https://www.hopkinsmedicine.org/health/treatment-tests-and-therapies/surgical-care

93. Book Text: *William Stewart Halsted* Link Associated with Text: https://en.wikipedia.org/wiki/William_Stewart_Halsted

94. Book Text: *Johns Hopkins University School of Medicine's* Link Associated with Text: https://www.hopkinsmedicine.org/som/index.html

95. Book Text: *Website Source of Quote3* Link Associated with Text: https://www.hopkinsmedicine.org/about/history/timeline/index.html#6

96. Book Text: *Video: How it Works: Bloodless Medicine and Surgery, An Alternative to Blood Transfusion* Link Associated with Text: https://www.youtube.com/watch?v=LmBX55IlAzg

97. Book Text: *Hopkins Department of Art as Applied to Medicine* Link Associated with Text: https://medicalart.johnshopkins.edu/

98. Book Text: *Max Broedel* Link Associated with Text: https://en.wikipedia.org/wiki/Max_Br%C3%B6del

99. Book Text: *Website Source of Quote4* Link Associated with Text: https://www.hopkinsmedicine.org/about/history/history7.html

100. Book Text: *Patient Check-Out Flowchart* Link Associated with Text: https://healthit.ahrq.gov/sites/default/files/docs/workflowtoolkit/Patient CheckOut.pdf

101. Book Text: *Personnel Department* Link Associated with Text: https://www.linkedin.com/pulse/historical-background-human-resource-management-vinaykumar-s

102. Book Text: *NCR* Link Associated with Text: https://en.wikipedia.org/wiki/NCR_Corporation

103. Book Text: *CIPD* Link Associated with Text: https://www.cipd.co.uk/about/who-we-are/history

104. Book Text: *Society for Human Resource Management (SHRM)* Link Associated with Text: https://www.shrm.org/about-shrm/Pages/default.aspx

105. Book Text: *Certified in Healthcare Human Resources (CHHR)* Link Associated with Text: http://learning.ashhra.org/CHHR_Study_Resources

106. Book Text: *healthcare human resources professional* Link Associated with Text: http://learning.ashhra.org/Files/Org/07b06170cefc43d8a4e6168d63fc03 62/site/AHA-CHHR-Handbook.pdf

107. Book Text: *Website Source of Quote5* Link Associated with Text: https://www.bls.gov/opub/btn/volume-5/healthcare-jobs-you-can-get-no-bachelors-degree.htm

108. Book Text: *state licensing of healthcare professionals* Link Associated with Text: https://cdn.mises.org/3_1_5_0.pdf

109. Book Text: *BLS* Link Associated with Text: https://www.bls.gov/home.htm

110. Book Text: *OOH* Link Associated with Text: https://www.bls.gov/ooh/home.htm

111. Book Text: *Healthcare Occupations* Link Associated with Text: https://www.bls.gov/ooh/healthcare/home.htm

112. Book Text: *(OSHA) for healthcare workers* Link Associated with Text: https://www.osha.gov/SLTC/healthcarefacilities/index.html

113. Book Text: *(NIOSH) for healthcare workers* Link Associated with Text: https://www.cdc.gov/niosh/topics/healthcare/default.html

114. Book Text: *Video: The Difference Between Respirators and Surgical Masks* Link Associated with Text: https://www.youtube.com/watch?v=ovSLAuY8ib8

115. Book Text: *smartdraw, Payroll Swim Lane Flowchart* Link Associated with Text: https://www.smartdraw.com/swim-lane-diagram/examples/payroll-swim-lane-flowchart/

116. Book Text: *Creately, Payroll Workflow Chart* Link Associated with Text: https://creately.com/diagram/example/il9j74wl/Payroll%20Workflow%20chart

117. Book Text: *Creately, HR Payroll Process Flow* Link Associated with Text: https://creately.com/diagram/example/i3yhkoyl/HR

118. Book Text: *Creately, Onboarding Flow Chart* Link Associated with Text: https://creately.com/diagram/example/inrv9geu1/Onboarding%20Flow%20Chart

119. Book Text: *Heflo Employee Onboarding* Link Associated with Text: https://www.heflo.com/blog/hr/employee-onboarding-process-flow-chart/

120. Book Text: *Creately, Human Resources* Link Associated with Text: https://creately.com/diagram/example/hcrtgzjx2/Human%20Resources

121. Book Text: *Creately, Human Resource Information System (Flowchart)* Link Associated with Text: https://creately.com/diagram/example/ihy1jrca/Human%20Resource%20Information%20System

122. Book Text: *TechnologyAdvice Human Resources Software Buyer's Guide* Link Associated with Text: https://technologyadvice.com/human-resources-software/

123. Book Text: *Human Resource Software* Link Associated with Text: https://www.capterra.com/human-resource-software/

124. Book Text: *Apptivo* Link Associated with Text: https://www.apptivo.com/

125. Book Text: *SimpleHRM* Link Associated with Text: https://sourceforge.net/projects/simplehrm/?utm_campaign=elearningindustry.com&utm_source=%2F9-free-human-resources-software-try&utm_medium=link

126. Book Text: *HR.my* Link Associated with Text: https://hr.my/

127. Book Text: *Chief Financial Officer (CFO)* Link Associated with Text: http://www.businessdictionary.com/definition/chief-financial-officer-CFO.html

128. Book Text: *The American Finance Association (AFA)* Link Associated with Text: https://www.afajof.org/

129. Book Text: *The Association for Finance Professionals (AFP)* Link Associated with Text: https://www.afponline.org/

130. Book Text: *The Professional Accounting Society of America (PASA)* Link Associated with Text: https://thepasa.org/

131. Book Text: *The American Accounting Association (AAA)* Link Associated with Text: http://aaahq.org/

132. Book Text: *HFMA* Link Associated with Text: https://www.hfma.org/about/

133. Book Text: *Certified Healthcare Financial Professional (CHFP)* Link Associated with Text: https://www.hfma.org/career-development/certifications/certified-healthcare-financial-professional.html

134. Book Text: *Lucidchart, Accounting Flowchart* Link Associated with Text: https://www.lucidchart.com/pages/templates/flowchart/accounting-flowchart-template
135. Book Text: *Creately, Accounting Process Flow (Flowchart)* Link Associated with Text: https://creately.com/diagram/example/hjkr44tl1/Accounting
136. Book Text: *Creately, Financial Reporting Cycle (Flowchart)* Link Associated with Text: https://creately.com/diagram/example/idgj1amm1/Financial%20Reporting%20Cycle
137. Book Text: *Financial Management Systems* Link Associated with Text: https://www.softwareadvice.com/erp/financial-management-system-comparison/
138. Book Text: *Financial Management Software* Link Associated with Text: https://www.capterra.com/financial-management-software/
139. Book Text: *GnuCash* Link Associated with Text: https://www.gnucash.org/
140. Book Text: *xTuple PostBooks* Link Associated with Text: https://xtuple.com/products/postbooks
141. Book Text: *ZipBooks* Link Associated with Text: https://zipbooks.com/
142. Book Text: *Wave* Link Associated with Text: https://www.waveapps.com/
143. Book Text: *history of money* Link Associated with Text: https://en.wikipedia.org/wiki/History_of_money
144. Book Text: *first coins used as money* Link Associated with Text: https://www.britishmuseum.org/collection/galleries/money
145. Book Text: *Lydians* Link Associated with Text: https://en.wikipedia.org/wiki/Lydia
146. Book Text: *United States dollar* Link Associated with Text: https://en.wikipedia.org/wiki/History_of_the_United_States_dollar
147. Book Text: *United States Treasury* Link Associated with Text: https://www.treasury.gov/about/history/Pages/edu_history_brochure.aspx
148. Book Text: *Alexander Hamilton* Link Associated with Text: https://en.wikipedia.org/wiki/Alexander_Hamilton
149. Book Text: *Bureau of Engraving and Printing (BEP)* Link Associated with Text: https://www.moneyfactory.gov/
150. Book Text: *United States Postal Service stamps* Link Associated with Text: https://en.wikipedia.org/wiki/Bureau_of_Engraving_and_Printing
151. Book Text: *United States Mint* Link Associated with Text: https://www.usmint.gov/about

152. Book Text: *independent government agency* Link Associated with Text: https://en.wikipedia.org/wiki/United_States_Mint

153. Book Text: *Fort Knox* Link Associated with Text: https://www.usmint.gov/about/mint-tours-facilities/fort-knox

154. Book Text: *Process and Functional Approaches in BPMN* Link Associated with Text: https://blog.goodelearning.com/subject-areas/bpmn/bpmn-what-are-functional-and-process-approaches/

155. Book Text: *with the Business Dictionary* Link Associated with Text: http://www.businessdictionary.com/definition/silo-mentality.html

156. Book Text: *Better Patient Flow Means Breaking Down the Silos* Link Associated with Text: http://www.ihi.org/resources/Pages/ImprovementStories/BetterPatientFlowMeansBreakingDowntheSilos.aspx

157. Book Text: *Breaking Down Silos to Improve Patient Flow, Hospital Efficiency* Link Associated with Text: https://www.beckershospitalreview.com/patient-flow/breaking-down-silos-to-improve-patient-flow-hospital-efficiency.html

158. Book Text: *Quashing the Silos and Getting to Integrated Health Care* Link Associated with Text: http://www.ncsl.org/blog/2014/11/12/quashing-the-silos-and-getting-to-integrated-health-care.aspx

159. Book Text: *Breaking Down Silos Is a Myth, Do This Instead* Link Associated with Text: https://www.inc.com/greg-satell/breaking-down-silos-is-a-myth-do-this-instead.html

160. Book Text: *The Need for a Team of Teams* Link Associated with Text: https://www.hhnmag.com/articles/3256-the-need-for-a-team-of-teams

161. Book Text: *It Takes a Team of Teams to Transform Healthcare* Link Associated with Text: https://www.emsworld.com/article/12264200/it-takes-a-team-of-teams-to-transform-healthcare

162. Book Text: *Fixing Healthcare Safety: Team of Teams* Link Associated with Text: https://patientsafe.wordpress.com/2017/02/09/team-of-teams/

163. Book Text: *first use of the term* Link Associated with Text: https://medium.com/business-process-management-software-comparisons/a-brief-history-of-process-management-to-the-modern-day-2f90d12d8e99

164. Book Text: *Gartner* Link Associated with Text: https://www.gartner.com/en

165. Book Text: *iBPMS* Link Associated with Text: https://www.gartner.com/reviews/market/intelligent-business-process-management-suites

166. Book Text: *Living Systems Process Suite (LSPS)* Link Associated with Text: https://www.whitestein.com/lsps-platform/lsps-overview

167. Book Text: *Creatio Studio* Link Associated with Text: https://www.bpmonline.com/studio

168. Book Text: *BP Logix* Link Associated with Text:
https://www.bplogix.com/

169. Book Text: *Genpact Cora* Link Associated with Text:
https://www.genpact.com/cora

170. Book Text: *Nintex* Link Associated with Text:
https://www.nintex.com/

171. Book Text: *jSonic BPM* Link Associated with Text:
http://jsonic.org/aboutjsonic

172. Book Text: *Activiti* Link Associated with Text:
https://www.activiti.org/

173. Book Text: *PMI* Link Associated with Text:
https://www.pmi.org/about/learn-about-pmi

174. Book Text: *offers a number of certificates* Link Associated with Text:
https://www.pmi.org/certifications/types

175. Book Text: *PMP* Link Associated with Text:
https://www.pmi.org/certifications/types/project-management-pmp

176. Book Text: *defines a project* Link Associated with Text:
https://www.pmi.org/about/learn-about-pmi/what-is-project-management

177. Book Text: *Top Project Management Excel Templates* Link Associated with Text: https://www.smartsheet.com/top-project-management-excel-templates

178. Book Text: *Free Project Management Templates* Link Associated with Text: https://www.projectmanager.com/templates

179. Book Text: *Asana Project Management Software* Link Associated with Text: https://asana.com/?noredirect

180. Book Text: *Workfront Enterprise Project Management Software* Link Associated with Text: https://www.workfront.com/

181. Book Text: *Zoho Project Management Software* Link Associated with Text: https://www.zoho.com/projects/

182. Book Text: *OpenProject* Link Associated with Text:
https://www.openproject.org/

183. Book Text: *ProjectOpen* Link Associated with Text:
http://www.project-open.com/en/products/editions.html

184. Book Text: *LibrePlan* Link Associated with Text:
https://www.libreplan.dev/

185. Book Text: *ProjectLibre* Link Associated with Text:
http://www.projectlibre.com/products

186. Book Text: *Business Process Management vs. Project Management: Differences You Need to Know* Link Associated with Text: https://www.processmaker.com/blog/bpm/business-process-management-vs-project-management/

187. Book Text: *defines strategic planning* Link Associated with Text:
http://www.businessdictionary.com/definition/strategic-planning.html

188. Book Text: *Mayo Clinic 2020 Initiative* Link Associated with Text: https://www.advisory.com/daily-briefing/2017/06/06/mayo-clinic

189. Book Text: *Massachusetts General Hospital ECOCH 2019-2021 Strategic Plan* Link Associated with Text: https://www.massgeneral.org/assets/MGH/pdf/ecoch/ECOCH%20Strategic%20Plan%20Report%2012.19.18.pdf

190. Book Text: *U.S. Department of Health and Human Services (HHS) Strategic Plan* Link Associated with Text: https://www.hhs.gov/about/strategic-plan/index.html

191. Book Text: *The American Dental Association (ADA) Strategic Plan* Link Associated with Text: https://www.ada.org/en/member-center/leadership-governance/strategic-planning

192. Book Text: *American Academy of Hospice and Palliative Medicine Strategic Plan (AAPHM) Strategic Plan* Link Associated with Text: http://aahpm.org/uploads/AAHPM20_Strategic_Plan3.pdf

193. Book Text: *Environmental Scanning* Link Associated with Text: http://www.businessdictionary.com/definition/environmental-scanning.html

194. Book Text: *SWOT Analysis* Link Associated with Text: http://www.businessdictionary.com/definition/SWOT-analysis.html

195. Book Text: *Video: Martin Reeves: Your Strategy Needs a Strategy* Link Associated with Text: https://www.youtube.com/watch?v=YE_ETgaFVo8

196. Book Text: *Free Strategic Planning Templates* Link Associated with Text: https://www.smartsheet.com/free-strategic-planning-templates

197. Book Text: *14 Free SWOT Analysis Templates* Link Associated with Text: https://www.smartsheet.com/14-free-swot-analysis-templates

198. Book Text: *StrategyShare* Link Associated with Text: https://www.strategyshare.com/

199. Book Text: *Cascade* Link Associated with Text: https://www.executestrategy.net/

200. Book Text: *Smartdraw* Link Associated with Text: https://www.smartdraw.com/strategic-planning/strategic-planning-software.htm

201. Book Text: *Envisio* Link Associated with Text: https://envisio.com/

202. Book Text: *Strategic Planning To Ensure Future Practice Success* Link Associated with Text: https://www.pharmacist.com/strategic-planning-ensure-future-practice-success

203. Book Text: *Why Strategic Planning is a Must for Practices* Link Associated with Text: http://www.physicianspractice.com/managers-administrators/why-strategic-planning-must-practices

204. Book Text: *Strategic Planning in Hospitals* Link Associated with Text: https://www.stratadecision.com/healthcare-and-hospital-strategic-planning/

205. Book Text: *5 Intangible Benefits Of Hospital Strategic Planning* Link Associated with Text: https://www.beckershospitalreview.com/strategic-planning/5-intangible-benefits-of-hospital-strategic-planning.html

206. Book Text: *6 Steps to Make Your Strategic Plan Really Strategic* Link Associated with Text: https://hbr.org/2018/08/6-steps-to-make-your-strategic-plan-really-strategic

207. Book Text: *Your Strategic Plans Probably Aren't Strategic, or Even Plans* Link Associated with Text: https://hbr.org/2018/04/your-strategic-plans-probably-arent-strategic-or-even-plans

208. Book Text: *All About Strategic Planning* Link Associated with Text: https://managementhelp.org/strategicplanning/index.htm

209. Book Text: *What Are The Basics Of Environmental Scanning as Part of the Strategic Planning Process?* Link Associated with Text: https://www.shrm.org/resourcesandtools/tools-and-samples/hr-qa/pages/basics-of-environmental-scanning.aspx

210. Book Text: *SWOT Analysis: What It Is and When to Use It* Link Associated with Text: https://www.businessnewsdaily.com/4245-swot-analysis.html

211. Book Text: *Writer* Link Associated with Text: https://www.libreoffice.org/discover/writer/

212. Book Text: *LibreOffice* Link Associated with Text: https://www.libreoffice.org/

213. Book Text: *Binding the Nation* Link Associated with Text: https://postalmuseum.si.edu/exhibits/current/binding-the-nation/index.html

214. Book Text: *Postal Service Act* Link Associated with Text: https://en.wikipedia.org/wiki/Postal_Service_Act

215. Book Text: *United States Postal Service: An American History 1775 – 2006* Link Associated with Text: https://about.usps.com/publications/pub100.pdf

216. Book Text: *Smithsonian National Postal Museum* Link Associated with Text: https://postalmuseum.si.edu/

217. Book Text: *United States Postmaster General (PMG)* Link Associated with Text: https://postalmuseum.si.edu/topics/us-postmasters-general

218. Book Text: *U.S. Postal Service* Link Associated with Text: http://about.usps.com/

219. Book Text: *United States Postal Inspection Service* Link Associated with Text: https://www.uspis.gov/

220. Book Text: *forerunner of this Service* Link Associated with Text: https://www.uspis.gov/about/history-of-uspis/

221. Book Text: *Chief Postal Inspector* Link Associated with Text: https://about.usps.com/who/leadership/officers/chief-pi.htm

222. Book Text: *William Goddard* Link Associated with Text: https://postalmuseum.si.edu/exhibition/behind-the-badge-postal-inspection-service-duties-and-history-history/william-goddard

223. Book Text: *Video: We are the U.S. Postal Inspection Service* Link Associated with Text: https://www.youtube.com/watch?v=Jrb2xb0ORXI

224. Book Text: *Video: Business Process Management (BPM) Explained in Under 5 Minutes* Link Associated with Text: https://www.youtube.com/watch?v=iI6T3-7JxdU

225. Book Text: *ABPD software* Link Associated with Text: https://www.bloorresearch.com/technology/automated-business-process-discovery-abpd/#whatitis

226. Book Text: *Minit* Link Associated with Text: https://www.minit.io/use-cases/process-discovery-and-process-mapping

227. Book Text: *Worksoft* Link Associated with Text: https://www.worksoft.com/

228. Book Text: *BPR* Link Associated with Text: http://www.businessdictionary.com/definition/business-process-reengineering-BPR.html

229. Book Text: *difference between* Link Associated with Text: https://kissflow.com/bpm/business-process-reengineering/

230. Book Text: *Michael M. Hammer* Link Associated with Text: https://en.wikipedia.org/wiki/Michael_Martin_Hammer

231. Book Text: *Reengineering Work: Don't Automate, Obliterate* Link Associated with Text: https://hbr.org/1990/07/reengineering-work-dont-automate-obliterate

232. Book Text: *Video: What's the Big Deal with Business Process Reengineering?* Link Associated with Text: https://www.youtube.com/watch?v=ee8iGNfem50

233. Book Text: *Business Process Re-engineering Application in Healthcare in a Relation to Health Information Systems* Link Associated with Text: https://www.sciencedirect.com/science/article/pii/S2212017313002600

234. Book Text: *Making Your Business More Competitive with Business Process Reengineering (BPR)* Link Associated with Text: https://www.cleverism.com/business-competitive-business-process-reengineering-bpr/

235. Book Text: *Business Process Reengineering in Healthcare: Literature Review on the Methodologies and Approaches* Link Associated with Text: https://www.researchgate.net/publication/292818143_Business_Process_Reengineering_in_Healthcare_Literature_Review_on_the_Methodologies_and_Approaches

236. Book Text: *defines research* Link Associated with Text: http://www.businessdictionary.com/definition/research.html

237. Book Text: *defines development* Link Associated with Text: http://www.businessdictionary.com/definition/development.html

238. Book Text: *defines innovation* Link Associated with Text: http://www.businessdictionary.com/definition/innovation.html

239. Book Text: *defines invention* Link Associated with Text: http://www.businessdictionary.com/definition/invention.html

240. Book Text: *Alexander Fleming* Link Associated with Text: https://www.acs.org/content/acs/en/education/whatischemistry/landmarks/flemingpenicillin.html

241. Book Text: *Abbott Laboratories* Link Associated with Text: https://www.abbott.com/

242. Book Text: *NCAUR* Link Associated with Text: https://www.ars.usda.gov/midwest-area/peoria-il/national-center-for-agricultural-utilization-research/docs/penicillin-opening-the-era-of-antibiotics/

243. Book Text: *First Use of Penicillin* Link Associated with Text: https://www.youtube.com/watch?v=rnrnLf9DjpA

244. Book Text: *John C. Sheehan* Link Associated with Text: https://en.wikipedia.org/wiki/John_C._Sheehan

245. Book Text: *Percy L. Spencer* Link Associated with Text: https://en.wikipedia.org/wiki/Percy_Spencer

246. Book Text: *Roy Plunkett* Link Associated with Text: https://en.wikipedia.org/wiki/Roy_J._Plunkett

247. Book Text: *Leo Baekeland* Link Associated with Text: https://en.wikipedia.org/wiki/Leo_Baekeland

248. Book Text: *Wilhelm Roentgen* Link Associated with Text: https://en.wikipedia.org/wiki/Wilhelm_R%C3%B6ntgen

249. Book Text: *Harry Coover* Link Associated with Text: https://en.wikipedia.org/wiki/Harry_Coover

250. Book Text: *Ira Remsen* Link Associated with Text: https://en.wikipedia.org/wiki/Ira_Remsen

251. Book Text: *Constantin Fahlberg* Link Associated with Text: https://www.sciencehistory.org/distillations/magazine/the-pursuit-of-sweet

252. Book Text: *Wilson Greatbatch* Link Associated with Text: https://lemelson.mit.edu/winners/wilson-greatbatch

253. Book Text: *Ratatouillle* Link Associated with Text: https://www.youtube.com/watch?v=b-brgtjwq4k

254. Book Text: *Penicillin's Discovery and Antibiotic Resistance: Lessons for the Future?* Link Associated with Text: https://www.ncbi.nlm.nih.gov/pmc/articles/PMC5369031/

255. Book Text: *The Real Story Behind Penicillin* Link Associated with Text: https://www.pbs.org/newshour/health/the-real-story-behind-the-worlds-first-antibiotic

256. Book Text: *A Brief History of the Antibiotic Era: Lessons Learned and Challenges for the Future* Link Associated with Text: https://www.ncbi.nlm.nih.gov/pmc/articles/PMC3109405/

257. Book Text: *The Enchanted Ring: The Untold Story of Penicillin* Link Associated with Text: https://mitpress.mit.edu/books/enchanted-ring

258. Book Text: *one of three categories* Link Associated with Text: https://differential.com/insights/the3typesofinnovation/

259. Book Text: *triage system* Link Associated with Text: https://www.ncbi.nlm.nih.gov/pmc/articles/PMC2564046/

260. Book Text: *Dominique Jean Larrey* Link Associated with Text: https://en.wikipedia.org/wiki/Dominique_Jean_Larrey

261. Book Text: *100 Objects That Shaped Public Health* Link Associated with Text: https://www.globalhealthnow.org/100-objects

262. Book Text: *20 Years of Healthcare Advances* Link Associated with Text: https://www.medscape.com/features/slideshow/20th-anniversary

263. Book Text: *support an organizational structure* Link Associated with Text: https://hbr.org/2015/04/the-5-requirements-of-a-truly-innovative-company

264. Book Text: *Cochrane* Link Associated with Text: http://www.cochrane.org/

265. Book Text: *systematic review* Link Associated with Text: https://consumers.cochrane.org/cochrane-and-systematic-reviews#systematic

266. Book Text: *Cochrane Library* Link Associated with Text: http://www.cochranelibrary.com/

267. Book Text: *International Association of Innovation Professionals (IAOIP)* Link Associated with Text: https://www.iaoip.org/

268. Book Text: *Successful Innovation through Business Process Management* Link Associated with Text: http://insights.btoes.com/business-transformation-operational-excellence/successful-innovation-through-business-process-management

269. Book Text: *What Has Innovation to Do with Business Process Management?* Link Associated with Text: http://www.dbizinstitute.org/resources/articles/what-has-innovation-do-business-process-management

270. Book Text: *Innovation as a Business Process* Link Associated with Text: http://www.bpminstitute.org/resources/articles/innovation-business-process

271. Book Text: *defines technology transfer* Link Associated with Text: http://www.businessdictionary.com/definition/technology-transfer.html

272. Book Text: *defines innovation diffusion* Link Associated with Text: http://www.businessdictionary.com/definition/diffusion-of-innovation.html

273. Book Text: *defines product adoption* Link Associated with Text: http://www.businessdictionary.com/definition/product-adoption-process.html

274. Book Text: *Gabriel Tarde* Link Associated with Text: https://en.wikipedia.org/wiki/Gabriel_Tarde

275. Book Text: *Everett Rogers* Link Associated with Text: https://en.wikipedia.org/wiki/Everett_Rogers

276. Book Text: *Diffusion of Innovations* Link Associated with Text: http://www.simonandschuster.com/books/Diffusion-of-Innovations-5th-Edition/Everett-M-Rogers/9780743222099

277. Book Text: *AUTM* Link Associated with Text: https://autm.net/

278. Book Text: *Bayh-Dole* Link Associated with Text: https://en.wikipedia.org/wiki/Bayh%E2%80%93Dole_Act

279. Book Text: *USPTO* Link Associated with Text: https://www.uspto.gov/about-us

280. Book Text: *established in 1802* Link Associated with Text: http://www.allgov.com/departments/department-of-commerce/united-states-patent-and-trademark-office?agencyid=7143#historycont

281. Book Text: *intellectual property* Link Associated with Text: https://en.wikipedia.org/wiki/Intellectual_property

282. Book Text: *Clause 8* Link Associated with Text: https://en.wikipedia.org/wiki/Copyright_Clause

283. Book Text: *clause states* Link Associated with Text: https://law.justia.com/constitution/us/article-1/50-copyrights-and-patents.html

284. Book Text: *Technology Transfer: From the Research Bench to Commercialization: Part 1: Intellectual Property Rights—Basics of Patents and Copyrights* Link Associated with Text: https://www.sciencedirect.com/science/article/pii/S2452302X17300037

285. Book Text: *Technology Transfer: From the Research Bench to Commercialization: Part 2: The Commercialization Process* Link Associated with Text: https://www.sciencedirect.com/science/article/pii/S2452302X17300529

286. Book Text: *Bayh-Dole Regulations* Link Associated with Text: https://grants.nih.gov/grants/bayh-dole.htm

287. Book Text: *Bayh-Dole Act: Everything You Need to Know* Link Associated with Text: https://www.upcounsel.com/bayh-dole-act

288. Book Text: *The Importance of the Bayh-Dole Act* Link Associated with Text: https://catalyst.phrma.org/the-importance-of-bayh-dole-act

289. Book Text: *The Patent Office Pony, A History of the Early Patent Office* Link Associated with Text: http://www.myoutbox.net/popstart.htm

290. Book Text: *Research America* Link Associated with Text: https://www.researchamerica.org/

291. Book Text: *U.S. Investments in Medical and Health Research and Development* Link Associated with Text: https://www.researchamerica.org/sites/default/files/RA-2017_InvestmentReport.pdf

292. Book Text: *Video: NIH: National Institutes of Health* Link Associated with Text: https://www.youtube.com/watch?v=ezpi8J1UQA0

293. Book Text: *Lyrica* Link Associated with Text: https://www.lyrica.com/

294. Book Text: *more than one billion dollars* Link Associated with Text: https://dailynorthwestern.com/2016/04/10/in-focus/in-focus-as-lyrica-profits-dry-up-northwestern-seeks-another-blockbuster-drug/

295. Book Text: *pregabalin* Link Associated with Text: https://en.wikipedia.org/wiki/Pregabalin#History

296. Book Text: *Richard Bruce Silverman* Link Associated with Text: https://en.wikipedia.org/wiki/Richard_Bruce_Silverman

297. Book Text: *Parke-Davis* Link Associated with Text: https://en.wikipedia.org/wiki/Parke-Davis

298. Book Text: *Warner-Lambert* Link Associated with Text: https://en.wikipedia.org/wiki/Warner%E2%80%93Lambert

299. Book Text: *Pfizer* Link Associated with Text: https://en.wikipedia.org/wiki/Pfizer

300. Book Text: *Pfizer company* Link Associated with Text: https://www.pfizer.com/

301. Book Text: *Medtronic* Link Associated with Text: http://www.medtronic.com/us-en/index.html

302. Book Text: *McKesson* Link Associated with Text: https://www.mckesson.com/

303. Book Text: *Center for Pharmacy Innovation and Outcomes (CPIO)* Link Associated with Text: https://www.geisinger.edu/research/departments-and-centers/pharmacy

304. Book Text: *Center for Primary Care Innovation* Link Associated with Text: https://www.feinberg.northwestern.edu/sites/cpci/

305. Book Text: *Innovation* Link Associated with Text: https://innovation.jefferson.edu/about.html

306. Book Text: *Accelerator Zone* Link Associated with Text: https://innovation.jefferson.edu/about/jefferson-accelerator-zone.html

307. Book Text: *Center for Innovative Pharmacy Solutions (CIPS)* Link Associated with Text: https://www.pharmacy.umaryland.edu/centers/cips/

308. Book Text: *Center for Health Innovation* Link Associated with Text: https://www.med.unc.edu/innovation/

309. Book Text: *Center for Health Care Innovation* Link Associated with Text: https://healthcareinnovation.upenn.edu/about

310. Book Text: *Kennedy Pharmacy Innovation Center* Link Associated with Text: https://sc.edu/study/colleges_schools/pharmacy/centers/kennedy_pharmacy_innovation_center/index.php

311. Book Text: *Innovation Centers (IC)* Link Associated with Text: http://cretdental.org/innovation-centers/

312. Book Text: *58 hospitals with innovation programs: 2017* Link Associated with Text: https://www.beckershospitalreview.com/lists/58-hospitals-and-health-systems-with-innovation-programs.html

313. Book Text: *Innovations* Link Associated with Text: https://innovations.clevelandclinic.org/About/Overview.aspx

314. Book Text: *Innovation Programs* Link Associated with Text: https://www.massgeneral.org/research/innovation-programs/

315. Book Text: *Center for Innovation (CFI)* Link Associated with Text: http://centerforinnovation.mayo.edu/

316. Book Text: *survey by Beckers* Link Associated with Text: https://www.beckershospitalreview.com/healthcare-information-technology/250-hospital-execs-rank-5-most-innovative-hospitals.html

317. Book Text: *Mayo Clinic* Link Associated with Text: https://www.mayoclinic.org/

318. Book Text: *Kaiser Permanente* Link Associated with Text: https://healthy.kaiserpermanente.org/

319. Book Text: *Cleveland Clinic* Link Associated with Text: https://my.clevelandclinic.org/

320. Book Text: *Geisinger Health System* Link Associated with Text: https://www.geisinger.org/

321. Book Text: *Intermountain Healthcare* Link Associated with Text: https://intermountainhealthcare.org/

322. Book Text: *collaboration between* Link Associated with Text: https://www.ada.org/en/press-room/news-releases/2017-archives/october/american-dental-association-joins-health-care-innovation-incubator-matter

323. Book Text: *MATTER* Link Associated with Text: https://matter.health/

324. Book Text: *Innovation Center* Link Associated with Text: https://www.ncpanct.org/innovation-center/about-the-ncpa-innovation-center

325. Book Text: *Healthcare Innovations Exchange* Link Associated with Text: https://innovations.ahrq.gov/about-us

326. Book Text: *Challenge.gov* Link Associated with Text: https://challenge.gov/

327. Book Text: *Innocentive* Link Associated with Text: https://www.innocentive.com/

328. Book Text: *Clayton M. Christiansen* Link Associated with Text: https://en.wikipedia.org/wiki/Clayton_M._Christensen

329. Book Text: *Disruptive Technologies: Catching the Wave* Link Associated with Text: https://hbr.org/1995/01/disruptive-technologies-catching-the-wave

330. Book Text: *Innovator's Dilemma: When New Technologies Cause Great Firms to Fail* Link Associated with Text: https://www.hbs.edu/faculty/Pages/item.aspx?num=46

331. Book Text: *Innovators Solution: The Innovator's Solution: Creating and Sustaining Successful Growth* Link Associated with Text: https://hbr.org/product/the-innovators-solution-creating-and-sustaining-successful-growth/16444E-KND-ENG

332. Book Text: *defines disruptive innovations* Link Associated with Text: https://hbr.org/2015/12/what-is-disruptive-innovation

333. Book Text: *The Innovator's Prescription: A Disruptive Solution for Health Care* Link Associated with Text: https://www.hbs.edu/faculty/Pages/item.aspx?num=35729

334. Book Text: *SOUNDVIEW Executive Book Summaries* Link Associated with Text: https://pdfs.semanticscholar.org/ff11/5d1c0bb616db41bbfed94572c01edddca5e2.pdf

335. Book Text: *Video: The Innovator's Prescription: A Disruptive Solution to Health Care* Link Associated with Text: https://www.youtube.com/watch?v=9DUKAGumqWw

336. Book Text: *Christiansen Institute Topics: Healthcare* Link Associated with Text: https://www.christenseninstitute.org/results/?_sft_topics=healthcare

337. Book Text: *How Disruption Can Finally Revolutionize Healthcare* Link Associated with Text: https://www.christenseninstitute.org/publications/how-disruption-can-finally-revolutionize-healthcare/

338. Book Text: *Will Disruptive Innovations Cure Health Care?* Link Associated with Text: https://hbr.org/2000/09/will-disruptive-innovations-cure-health-care

339. Book Text: *Harnessing Disruptive Innovation in Health Care* Link Associated with Text: https://innovations.ahrq.gov/perspectives/harnessing-disruptive-innovation-health-care

340. Book Text: *Disruptive Innovation In Health Care Delivery: A Framework For Business-Model Innovation* Link Associated with Text: https://www.healthaffairs.org/doi/10.1377/hlthaff.27.5.1329

341. Book Text: *Is health care ready for disruptive innovation? (part one)*
      Link Associated with Text: https://hpnonline.org/is-health-care-ready-for-disruptive-innovation-part-one/

342. Book Text: *Is health care ready for disruptive innovation? (part two)*
      Link Associated with Text: https://hpnonline.org/is-health-care-ready-for-disruptive-innovation-part-two/

343. Book Text: *Is health care ready for disruptive innovation? (part three)*
      Link Associated with Text: https://hpnonline.org/is-health-care-ready-for-disruptive-innovation-part-three/

344. Book Text: *New Marketplace Survey: The Sources of Health Care Innovation* Link Associated with Text:
      https://catalyst.nejm.org/disruptive-innovation-in-healthcare-survey/

345. Book Text: *5 Ways to Drive Disruptive Innovation in Healthcare* Link Associated with Text: https://www.inc.com/soren-kaplan/5-ways-to-drive-disruptive-innovation-in-healthcar.html

346. Book Text: *CHS* Link Associated with Text: http://www.chs.net/

347. Book Text: *of a portion of the organization* Link Associated with Text: http://www.chs.net/quorum-health-corporation/

348. Book Text: *QHC* Link Associated with Text:
      http://www.quorumhealth.com/

349. Book Text: *defines as* Link Associated with Text:
      http://www.businessdictionary.com/definition/entrepreneurship.html

350. Book Text: *Antheia* Link Associated with Text: https://antheia.bio/

351. Book Text: *Stanford University* Link Associated with Text:
      http://med.stanford.edu/news/all-news/2018/04/researchers-engineer-yeast-to-manufacture-complex-medicine.html

352. Book Text: *Sapience Therapeutics* Link Associated with Text:
      https://www.sapiencetherapeutics.com/about

353. Book Text: *Columbia University* Link Associated with Text:
      https://techventures.columbia.edu/news-and-events/latest-news/sapience-therapeutics-selected-winner-jlabs-nyc-quickfire-challenge

354. Book Text: *Synlogic* Link Associated with Text:
      https://www.synlogictx.com/about/about-us/

355. Book Text: *Massachusetts Institute of Technology (MIT)* Link Associated with Text: http://news.mit.edu/2016/startup-synlogic-reprogramming-gut-bacteria-living-therapeutics-0405

356. Book Text: *more than 80 spin-off companies* Link Associated with Text: https://www.scripps.edu/technology-development/initiatives/spin-off-companies/

357. Book Text: *OTD* Link Associated with Text:
      https://www.scripps.edu/technology-development/

358. Book Text: *Ambient Clinical Analytics* Link Associated with Text:
      https://ambientclinical.com/about/

359. Book Text: *Mayo Clinic (Ventures)* Link Associated with Text: http://ventures.mayoclinic.org/impact/leveraging-it-for-safety.php

360. Book Text: *Centerline Biomedical* Link Associated with Text: https://www.centerlinebiomedical.com/about-us/

361. Book Text: *Cleveland Clinic (Ventures)* Link Associated with Text: https://ventures.clevelandclinic.org/Cleveland-Clinic-Ventures/Ventures-Portfolio

362. Book Text: *Navican* Link Associated with Text: https://intermountainhealthcare.org/about/who-we-are/trustee-resource-center/newsletter/newsletter-archive/navican-opens-precision-cancer-care-center-in-downtown-salt-lake-city/

363. Book Text: *Intermountain Healthcare (Ventures)* Link Associated with Text: https://intermountainhealthcare.org/about/transforming-healthcare/innovation/business-development/

364. Book Text: *defines a business incubator* Link Associated with Text: http://www.businessdictionary.com/definition/business-incubator.html

365. Book Text: *12 healthcare startup incubators and accelerators to know* Link Associated with Text: https://www.beckershospitalreview.com/healthcare-information-technology/12-healthcare-startup-incubators-and-accelerators-to-know.html

366. Book Text: *Ultimate List of Medical Device Incubators and Accelerators (50+)* Link Associated with Text: https://www.greenlight.guru/blog/medical-device-incubators-accelerators

367. Book Text: *Digital Health Accelerators* Link Associated with Text: https://www.digital.health/digital-health-accelerators

368. Book Text: *Top 17 Health Startup Accelerators* Link Associated with Text: https://www.medicalstartups.org/top/accelerator/

369. Book Text: *How Healthcare Spin-Offs are Affecting the Industry* Link Associated with Text: http://www.managedhealthcareexecutive.com/business-strategy/how-healthcare-spin-offs-are-affecting-industry

370. Book Text: *The Top Resources For Healthcare Entrepreneurs, In Every Category.* Link Associated with Text: https://medium.com/@mikettownsend/the-top-resources-for-healthcare-entrepreneurs-in-every-category-b35603cac094

371. Book Text: *What is a pitch deck?* Link Associated with Text: https://pitchdeck.improvepresentation.com/what-is-a-pitch-deck

372. Book Text: *Pitch Deck Examples* Link Associated with Text: https://pitchdeckexamples.com/

373. Book Text: *Lessons From The Early Pitch Decks Of AirBnB, BuzzFeed, And YouTube* Link Associated with Text: https://www.fastcompany.com/3050985/lessons-from-the-early-pitch-decks-of-airbnb-buzzfeed-and-youtube

374. Book Text: *30 Legendary Startup Pitch Decks And What You Can Learn From Them* Link Associated with Text: https://piktochart.com/blog/startup-pitch-decks-what-you-can-learn/

375. Book Text: *defines a business plan* Link Associated with Text: http://www.businessdictionary.com/definition/business-plan.html

376. Book Text: *Write your business plan* Link Associated with Text: https://www.sba.gov/business-guide/plan-your-business/write-your-business-plan

377. Book Text: *7 Steps to a Perfectly Written Business Plan* Link Associated with Text: https://www.entrepreneur.com/article/281416

378. Book Text: *How to Write the Perfect Business Plan: A Comprehensive Guide* Link Associated with Text: https://www.inc.com/jeff-haden/how-to-write-perfect-business-plan-a-comprehensive-guide.html

379. Book Text: *What is the Difference Between a Business Plan and a Strategic Plan?* Link Associated with Text: https://onstrategyhq.com/resources/what-is-the-difference-between-a-business-plan-and-a-strategic-plan/

380. Book Text: *Pitch Deck vs. Business Plan: The Differences and Uses of Each* Link Associated with Text: https://pitchdeckfire.com/resources/pitch-deck-vs-business-plan-the-differences-and-uses-of-each/

381. Book Text: *ticker tape* Link Associated with Text: https://en.wikipedia.org/wiki/Ticker_tape

382. Book Text: *NYSE* Link Associated with Text: https://www.nyse.com/index

383. Book Text: *ticker tape parades* Link Associated with Text: https://en.wikipedia.org/wiki/Ticker_tape_parade

384. Book Text: *useful ticker tape* Link Associated with Text: http://www.investopedia.com/articles/01/070401.asp

385. Book Text: *introduced his Universal Stock Ticker* Link Associated with Text: http://edison.rutgers.edu/ticker.htm

386. Book Text: *Edward Calahan* Link Associated with Text: https://en.wikipedia.org/wiki/Edward_A._Calahan

387. Book Text: *power naps* Link Associated with Text: https://en.wikipedia.org/wiki/Power_nap

388. Book Text: *Thomas Edison & The History of Electricity* Link Associated with Text: https://www.ge.com/about-us/history/thomas-edison

389. Book Text: *Thomas A. Edison Papers* Link Associated with Text: http://edison.rutgers.edu/

390. Book Text: *Thomas Edison, Wikipedia* Link Associated with Text: https://en.wikipedia.org/wiki/Thomas_Edison

391. Book Text: *37 Quotes From Thomas Edison That Will Inspire Success* Link Associated with Text: https://www.inc.com/kevin-daum/37-quotes-from-thomas-edison-that-will-bring-out-your-best.html

392. Book Text: *Thomas Edison National Historical Park* Link Associated with Text: https://www.nps.gov/edis/index.htm

393. Book Text: *Edison's Laboratory* Link Associated with Text: https://www.nps.gov/edis/learn/historyculture/collections.htm

394. Book Text: *Glenmont* Link Associated with Text: https://www.nps.gov/edis/learn/historyculture/glenmont-collections.htm

395. Book Text: *National Historic Chemical Landmark* Link Associated with Text: https://www.acs.org/content/acs/en/education/whatischemistry/landmarks/thomas-edison.html

396. Book Text: *Video: Thomas Edison National Historical Park Educational Video* Link Associated with Text: https://www.youtube.com/watch?v=Cf_0L0nIhrI

397. Book Text: *ONC* Link Associated with Text: https://www.healthit.gov/topic/about-onc

398. Book Text: *distinction between* Link Associated with Text: https://www.healthit.gov/buzz-blog/electronic-health-and-medical-records/emr-vs-ehr-difference/

399. Book Text: *Health IT Playbook* Link Associated with Text: https://www.healthit.gov/playbook/

400. Book Text: *three major data exchange* Link Associated with Text: https://www.healthit.gov/faq/what-are-different-types-health-information-exchange

401. Book Text: *interoperability* Link Associated with Text: https://www.healthit.gov/topic/interoperability

402. Book Text: *Precision Medicine Initiative (PMI)* Link Associated with Text: https://www.healthit.gov/topic/scientific-initiatives/precision-medicine

403. Book Text: *Sync for Science (S4S)* Link Associated with Text: http://syncfor.science/

404. Book Text: *Sync for Genes (S4G)* Link Associated with Text: http://www.sync4genes.org/

405. Book Text: *All of Us Research Program* Link Associated with Text: https://allofus.nih.gov/about

406. Book Text: *SNOMED-CT* Link Associated with Text: https://www.nlm.nih.gov/healthit/snomedct/

407. Book Text: *Health Level Seven (HL7)* Link Associated with Text: http://www.hl7.org/implement/standards/

408. Book Text: *ISA* Link Associated with Text: https://www.healthit.gov/isa/

409. Book Text: *ISA Reference Edition* Link Associated with Text: https://www.healthit.gov/isa/sites/isa/files/2018%20ISA%20Reference%20Edition.pdf

410.   Book Text: *Video: Introduction to HL7 and Interfaces in Healthcare* Link Associated with Text:
https://www.youtube.com/watch?v=T6dZOPHe2Jc

411.   Book Text: *ONC Interoperability Basics* Link Associated with Text:
https://www.healthit.gov/public-course/interoperability-basics-training/HITRC_lsn1069/wrap_menupage.htm

412.   Book Text: *ONC Interoperability Roadmap* Link Associated with Text: https://www.healthit.gov/topic/interoperability/interoperability-roadmap

413.   Book Text: *Electronic health records: What will it take to make them work?* Link Associated with Text: https://news.aamc.org/patient-care/article/electronic-health-records-what-will-it-take/

414.   Book Text: *HITECH* Link Associated with Text:
https://www.cdc.gov/ehrmeaningfuluse/introduction.html

415.   Book Text: *PI* Link Associated with Text:
https://www.cms.gov/Regulations-and-Guidance/Legislation/EHRIncentivePrograms/index.html?redirect=/EHRIncentivePrograms

416.   Book Text: *Health IT Certification Program* Link Associated with Text: https://www.healthit.gov/topic/certification-ehrs/certification-health-it

417.   Book Text: *CMS Stage 1 MU Final Rule* Link Associated with Text:
http://www.gpo.gov/fdsys/pkg/FR-2010-07-28/pdf/2010-17210.pdf

418.   Book Text: *ONC Stage 1 MU Final Rule* Link Associated with Text:
http://www.gpo.gov/fdsys/pkg/FR-2010-07-28/pdf/2010-17207.pdf

419.   Book Text: *CMS Stage 2 MU Final Rule* Link Associated with Text:
http://www.gpo.gov/fdsys/pkg/FR-2012-09-04/pdf/2012-21050.pdf

420.   Book Text: *ONC Stage 2 MU Final Rule* Link Associated with Text:
http://www.gpo.gov/fdsys/pkg/FR-2012-09-04/pdf/2012-20982.pdf

421.   Book Text: *CMS Modified Stage 2 and Stage 3 Final Rule* Link Associated with Text: https://www.gpo.gov/fdsys/pkg/FR-2015-10-16/pdf/2015-25595.pdf

422.   Book Text: *ONC Modified Stage 2 and Stage 3 Final Rule* Link Associated with Text: https://www.gpo.gov/fdsys/pkg/FR-2015-10-16/pdf/2015-25597.pdf

423.   Book Text: *ONC Interoperability Training Courses* Link Associated with Text: https://www.healthit.gov/topic/interoperability-training-courses

424.   Book Text: *ONC Tech Lab's Interoperability in Action Webinar Series* Link Associated with Text:
https://www.healthit.gov/topic/interoperability/about-onc-tech-labs-interoperability-action-webinar-series

425.   Book Text: *Health Insurance Portability and Accountability Act* Link Associated with Text: https://www.hhs.gov/hipaa/index.html

426. Book Text: *Privacy, Security, and HIPAA* Link Associated with Text: https://www.healthit.gov/topic/privacy-security-and-hipaa
427. Book Text: *Patient Consent for Electronic Health Information Exchange* Link Associated with Text: https://www.healthit.gov/topic/patient-consent-electronic-health-information-exchange
428. Book Text: *Patient Consent for Electronic Health Information Exchange and Interoperability* Link Associated with Text: https://www.healthit.gov/topic/interoperability/patient-consent-electronic-health-information-exchange-and-interoperability
429. Book Text: *Health Information Exchange: What do patients want?* Link Associated with Text: http://journals.sagepub.com/doi/abs/10.1177/1460458216647190
430. Book Text: *Who Owns Health Information?* Link Associated with Text: http://www.healthinfolaw.org/lb/download-document/6640/field_article_file
431. Book Text: *Who Really Owns Your Health Data?* Link Associated with Text: https://www.forbes.com/sites/forbestechcouncil/2018/04/23/who-really-owns-your-health-data/#58b1eb256d62
432. Book Text: *Henry Stanley Plummer* Link Associated with Text: http://history.mayoclinic.org/historic-highlights/diversified-genius.php
433. Book Text: *Homer R. Warner* Link Associated with Text: https://en.wikipedia.org/wiki/Homer_R._Warner
434. Book Text: *Homer Warner Center for Informatics Research* Link Associated with Text: https://intermountainhealthcare.org/about/transforming-healthcare/innovation/medical-informatics/about-us/
435. Book Text: *Video: Intermountain Medical Center: Homer Warner Center for Informatics Research* Link Associated with Text: https://www.youtube.com/watch?v=t45AN-AgOgM
436. Book Text: *Regenstrief Institute* Link Associated with Text: https://www.regenstrief.org/centers/center-biomedical-informatics/
437. Book Text: *Clement McDonald* Link Associated with Text: https://lhncbc.nlm.nih.gov/personnel/clem-mcdonald
438. Book Text: *London Bills of Mortality* Link Associated with Text: https://en.wikipedia.org/wiki/Bills_of_mortality
439. Book Text: *Bertillon List of Causes of Death* Link Associated with Text: https://archive.org/details/bertillonclassif00amer/page/4
440. Book Text: *Jacques Bertillon* Link Associated with Text: http://www-history.mcs.st-andrews.ac.uk/Biographies/Bertillon.html
441. Book Text: *ISI* Link Associated with Text: https://www.isi-web.org/index.php
442. Book Text: *APHA* Link Associated with Text: https://www.apha.org/

443. Book Text: *International List of Causes of Death* Link Associated with Text:
https://www.cdc.gov/nchs/data/misc/classification_diseases2011.pdf
444. Book Text: *responsibility was transferred* Link Associated with Text:
http://www.who.int/classifications/icd/en/
445. Book Text: *as implemented in the United States* Link Associated with Text: https://www.cdc.gov/nchs/icd/index.htm
446. Book Text: *NCHS* Link Associated with Text:
https://www.cdc.gov/nchs/index.htm
447. Book Text: *CDC* Link Associated with Text: https://www.cdc.gov/
448. Book Text: *(HCPCS) Level II* Link Associated with Text:
https://www.cms.gov/Medicare/Coding/MedHCPCSGenInfo/HCPCSC
ODINGPROCESS.html
449. Book Text: *CMS* Link Associated with Text: https://www.cms.gov/
450. Book Text: *CPT* Link Associated with Text: https://www.ama-assn.org/practice-management/cpt-current-procedural-terminology
451. Book Text: *AMA* Link Associated with Text: https://www.ama-assn.org/
452. Book Text: *AAPC* Link Associated with Text: https://www.aapc.com/
453. Book Text: *certifications* Link Associated with Text:
https://www.aapc.com/certification/
454. Book Text: *CPC* Link Associated with Text:
https://www.aapc.com/certification/cpc/
455. Book Text: *AHIMA* Link Associated with Text:
http://www.ahima.org/
456. Book Text: *many certifications* Link Associated with Text:
http://www.ahima.org/certification
457. Book Text: *CCS* Link Associated with Text:
http://www.ahima.org/certification/CCS
458. Book Text: *Practice Management Institute (PMI)* Link Associated with Text: https://www.pmimd.com/
459. Book Text: *offers certifications* Link Associated with Text:
https://www.pmimd.com/certifications/
460. Book Text: *CMC* Link Associated with Text:
https://www.pmimd.com/certifications/certification.php?id=119
461. Book Text: *Workflow Process Mapping for Electronic Health Record (EHR) Implementation* Link Associated with Text:
https://www.healthit.gov/resource/workflow-process-mapping-electronic-health-record-ehr-implementation
462. Book Text: *Practice Transformation Toolkit* Link Associated with Text: https://www.healthit.gov/resource/practice-transformation-toolkit
463. Book Text: *VISTA* Link Associated with Text:
https://en.wikipedia.org/wiki/VistA

464. Book Text: *VA Software Document Library* Link Associated with Text: https://www.va.gov/vdl/
465. Book Text: *WorldVistA* Link Associated with Text: http://worldvista.org/
466. Book Text: *OSEHRA* Link Associated with Text: https://www.linkedin.com/company/osehra
467. Book Text: *to replace VistA* Link Associated with Text: https://www.healthcareitnews.com/news/va-picks-cerner-replace-vista-trump-says-ehr-will-fix-agencys-data-sharing-once-and-all
468. Book Text: *MHS Genesis* Link Associated with Text: https://health.mil/mhsgenesis
469. Book Text: *Cerner's Millennium* Link Associated with Text: https://www.cerner.com/se/en/solutions/millennium
470. Book Text: *Hospitals & Health Systems* Link Associated with Text: https://www.cerner.com/solutions/health-systems
471. Book Text: *actually hurts* Link Associated with Text: https://www.pbs.org/newshour/health/doctors-think-electronic-health-records-hurting-relationships-patients
472. Book Text: *Poll: Doctors say electronic health records need overhaul* Link Associated with Text: https://scopeblog.stanford.edu/2018/06/04/poll-doctors-say-electronic-health-records-need-overhaul/
473. Book Text: *DoD and VA Update: Early Results, Fine-tuning and Next Steps* Link Associated with Text: https://www.cerner.com/blog/dod-va-update-early-results-fine-tuning
474. Book Text: *Measuring Performance Directly Using the Veterans Health Administration Electronic Medical Record: A Comparison With External Peer Review* Link Associated with Text: https://www.ncbi.nlm.nih.gov/pmc/articles/PMC3460379/
475. Book Text: *Utilizing patient data from the veterans administration electronic health record to support web-based clinical decision support: informatics challenges and issues from three clinical domains* Link Associated with Text: https://www.ncbi.nlm.nih.gov/pmc/articles/PMC5517800/
476. Book Text: *What Health Systems, Hospitals, and Physicians Need to Know About Implementing Electronic Health Records* Link Associated with Text: https://hbr.org/2017/06/what-health-systems-hospitals-and-physicians-need-to-know-about-implementing-electronic-health-records
477. Book Text: *Kareo Go Practice Demo EMR/EHR Videos* Link Associated with Text: https://www.kareo.com/ehr/demos
478. Book Text: *OpenEMR Demos* Link Associated with Text: https://www.open-emr.org/demo/
479. Book Text: *Controlled Substances Act* Link Associated with Text: https://en.wikipedia.org/wiki/Controlled_Substances_Act

480. Book Text: *(DEA) the authority to place* Link Associated with Text: https://www.dea.gov/drug-scheduling
481. Book Text: *RxBenefit Clarity* Link Associated with Text: https://www.mckesson.com/pharmacy-management/patient-care/benefit-information/
482. Book Text: *RelayHealth Pharmacy Solutions* Link Associated with Text: https://www.mckesson.com/about-mckesson/our-company/businesses/relayhealth/
483. Book Text: *CoverMyMeds* Link Associated with Text: https://www.covermymeds.com/main/
484. Book Text: *SureScripts* Link Associated with Text: https://surescripts.com/
485. Book Text: *Electronic Prior Authorization* Link Associated with Text: https://surescripts.com/enhance-prescribing/prior-authorization/
486. Book Text: *Real-Time Prescription Benefit* Link Associated with Text: https://surescripts.com/enhance-prescribing/benefit-optimization/
487. Book Text: *CVS Health* Link Associated with Text: https://cvshealth.com/
488. Book Text: *CVS Caremark* Link Associated with Text: https://www.caremark.com/wps/portal/!ut/p/z1/04_Sj9CPykssy0xPLMnMz0vMAfIjo8zinSzMzS28gwxDXQJ8DAw8zYxdfTwMXYwNDAz0wwkpiMIvHUlIf0FuRCUAmpEFWQ!!/
489. Book Text: *DEA: The Controlled Substances Act* Link Associated with Text: https://www.dea.gov/controlled-substances-act
490. Book Text: *FDA: Drugs* Link Associated with Text: https://www.fda.gov/drugs
491. Book Text: *defines E-Prescribing* Link Associated with Text: https://www.cms.gov/Medicare/E-Health/Eprescribing/index.html
492. Book Text: *Preventing Medication Errors: Quality Chasm Series* Link Associated with Text: https://psnet.ahrq.gov/issue/preventing-medication-errors-quality-chasm-series
493. Book Text: *MDtoolbox E-Prescribing* Link Associated with Text: https://mdtoolbox.com/
494. Book Text: *EPCS compliant* Link Associated with Text: https://mdtoolbox.com/eprescribe-controlled-substances.aspx
495. Book Text: *(DEA) in 2010* Link Associated with Text: https://www.deadiversion.usdoj.gov/fed_regs/rules/2020/fr0421_3.htm
496. Book Text: *E-Prescribing Enables Pharmacists to Improve Medication Adherence* Link Associated with Text: https://www.mckesson.com/blog/the-impact-of-e-prescribing/
497. Book Text: *AAFP - Electronic Prescribing of Controlled Substances (EPCS)* Link Associated with Text: https://www.aafp.org/practice-management/health-it/epcs.html
498. Book Text: *Pharmacy Management System* Link Associated with Text: https://www.mckesson.com/pharmacy-management/software/

499. Book Text: *CVS Minute Clinic* Link Associated with Text: https://www.cvs.com/minuteclinic

500. Book Text: *CVS Health Transform Care* Link Associated with Text: https://payorsolutions.cvshealth.com/programs-and-services/transform-care

501. Book Text: *CVS Health Transform Diabetes Care* Link Associated with Text: https://payorsolutions.cvshealth.com/programs-and-services/transform-care/transform-diabetes-care

502. Book Text: *CVS Health Transform Rheumatoid Arthritis Care* Link Associated with Text: https://payorsolutions.cvshealth.com/programs-and-services/transform-care/transform-rheumatoid-arthritis-care

503. Book Text: *done by pharmacies and pharmacists* Link Associated with Text: https://www.pharmacist.com/sites/default/files/files/core_elements_of_an_mtm_practice.pdf

504. Book Text: *more than 115 people* Link Associated with Text: https://www.drugabuse.gov/drugs-abuse/opioids/opioid-overdose-crisis

505. Book Text: *prescription opioid* Link Associated with Text: https://www.hhs.gov/opioids/about-the-epidemic/index.html

506. Book Text: *SUPPORT* Link Associated with Text: https://www.congress.gov/115/bills/hr6/BILLS-115hr6enr.pdf

507. Book Text: *PDMP* Link Associated with Text: https://www.healthit.gov/playbook/opioid-epidemic-and-health-it/

508. Book Text: *Video: The Science of Opioids* Link Associated with Text: https://www.youtube.com/watch?v=AqDo4LiKz-c

509. Book Text: *Making Progress in the Fight Against Opioid Misuse and Abuse* Link Associated with Text: https://cvshealth.com/thought-leadership/making-progress-in-the-fight-against-opioid-misuse-and-abuse

510. Book Text: *OPIOIDS* Link Associated with Text: https://surescripts.com/news-center/intelligence-in-action/opioids/

511. Book Text: *Opioid Crisis* Link Associated with Text: https://www.hrsa.gov/opioids

512. Book Text: *Opioid Overdose* Link Associated with Text: https://www.cdc.gov/drugoverdose/index.html

513. Book Text: *Four Ways Pharmacists Are Fighting Opioid Abuse* Link Associated with Text: http://www.drugtopics.com/latest/four-ways-pharmacists-are-fighting-opioid-abuse

514. Book Text: *What States Need to Know about PDMPs* Link Associated with Text: https://www.cdc.gov/drugoverdose/pdmp/states.html

515. Book Text: *Purdue Phama - Open Letter* Link Associated with Text: https://www.purduepharma.com/news-media/perspectives/open-letter/

516. Book Text: *15 percent of dental practices* Link Associated with Text: https://www.himss.org/news/dental-informatics-insights

517. Book Text: *advantage of some of the incentives* Link Associated with Text: https://www.ada.org/en/member-center/member-benefits/practice-resources/dental-informatics/electronic-health-records/ehr-faq-index/medicaid-and-medicare-ehr-incentive-program-faq-not-in-matrix/general-ehr-incentive-program-questions-not-in-matrix

518. Book Text: *ACE Dental* Link Associated with Text: https://www.ace-dental.com/

519. Book Text: *Curve Dental* Link Associated with Text: https://www.curvedental.com/

520. Book Text: *iDental Soft* Link Associated with Text: https://www.identalsoft.com/

521. Book Text: *Planet DDS Denticon* Link Associated with Text: https://www.planetdds.com/

522. Book Text: *Tab32* Link Associated with Text: http://www.tab32.com/

523. Book Text: *American Dental Association (ADA): Electronic Health Records* Link Associated with Text: https://www.ada.org/en/member-center/member-benefits/practice-resources/dental-informatics/electronic-health-records

524. Book Text: *Weighing the Challenges and Benefits of Dental EHRs* Link Associated with Text: https://www.dmdtoday.com/news/weighing-the-challenges-and-benefits-of-dental-ehrs

525. Book Text: *Clinical Documentation of Dental Care in an Era of EHR Use* Link Associated with Text: https://www.ncbi.nlm.nih.gov/pmc/articles/PMC5119920/

526. Book Text: *Five of the best dentistry EHRs* Link Associated with Text: https://www.ehrinpractice.com/best-dentistry-ehrs.html

527. Book Text: *Dental Software* Link Associated with Text: https://www.softwareadvice.com/dental/

528. Book Text: *Dental Practice Software* Link Associated with Text: https://www.capterra.com/dental-software/

529. Book Text: *Video: Exploring the History of Teeth at Baltimore's Dentistry Museum* Link Associated with Text: https://www.youtube.com/watch?v=YHiPuRiKWwE

530. Book Text: *Dr. Samuel D. Harris National Museum of Dentistry* Link Associated with Text: http://www.dental.umaryland.edu/museum/

531. Book Text: *PHR* Link Associated with Text: https://www.healthit.gov/faq/what-personal-health-record-0

532. Book Text: *PHRs* Link Associated with Text: https://www.healthit.gov/topic/health-it-basics/frequently-asked-questions

533. Book Text: *two types* Link Associated with Text: https://www.healthit.gov/sites/default/files/about-phrs-for-providers-011311.pdf

534. Book Text: *(AHIMA) MyPHR* Link Associated with Text:
http://www.myphr.com/StartaPHR/what_is_a_phr.aspx
535. Book Text: *Choose a PHR* Link Associated with Text:
http://www.myphr.com/resources/choose.aspx
536. Book Text: *MyPHR video library* Link Associated with Text:
http://myphr.com/Tools/phrvideos.aspx
537. Book Text: *MyHealthEData Initiative* Link Associated with Text:
https://www.cms.gov/newsroom/press-releases/cms-finalizes-changes-empower-patients-and-reduce-administrative-burden
538. Book Text: *Initiative* Link Associated with Text:
https://www.cms.gov/newsroom/fact-sheets/trump-administration-announces-myhealthedata-initiative-himss18
539. Book Text: *One component* Link Associated with Text:
https://www.healthdataanswers.net/cms-blue-button-2-0-now-available-part-myhealthedata/
540. Book Text: *Blue Button* Link Associated with Text:
https://www.medicare.gov/manage-your-health/medicares-blue-button-blue-button-20
541. Book Text: *Blue Button 2.0* Link Associated with Text:
https://bluebutton.cms.gov/#getting-started
542. Book Text: *What are the benefits of personal health records?* Link Associated with Text: https://www.healthit.gov/faq/what-are-benefits-personal-health-records
543. Book Text: *Electronic Health Records Infographic* Link Associated with Text: https://www.healthit.gov/infographic/electronic-health-records-infographic
544. Book Text: *Why consumers want their health records* Link Associated with Text: https://rockhealth.com/why-consumers-want-their-health-records/
545. Book Text: *Video: MyHealthEData* Link Associated with Text:
https://www.youtube.com/watch?v=2DCeCdU1PeE
546. Book Text: *William Oughtred* Link Associated with Text:
http://www.computinghistory.org.uk/det/5922/Slide-Rule-invented-by-William-Oughtred/
547. Book Text: *William Oughtred, Wikipedia* Link Associated with Text:
https://en.wikipedia.org/wiki/William_Oughtred
548. Book Text: *About Slide Rules* Link Associated with Text:
http://www.hpmuseum.org/sliderul.htm
549. Book Text: *Slide Rule, Wikipedia* Link Associated with Text:
https://en.wikipedia.org/wiki/Slide_rule
550. Book Text: *What Can You Do With A Slide Rule?* Link Associated with Text: http://www.math.utah.edu/~pa/sliderules/
551. Book Text: *The Slide Rule: A Computing Device That Put A Man On The Moon* Link Associated with Text:

https://www.npr.org/sections/ed/2014/10/22/356937347/the-slide-rule-a-computing-device-that-put-a-man-on-the-moon

552. Book Text: *Massachusetts Institute of Technology (MIT) Museum* Link Associated with Text: https://mitmuseum.mit.edu/

553. Book Text: *museum contains* Link Associated with Text: https://webmuseum.mit.edu/main.php?module=objects

554. Book Text: *MIT Museum Studio* Link Associated with Text: https://mitmuseum.mit.edu/mit-community/mit-museum-studio-and-compton-gallery

555. Book Text: *Slide Rules* Link Associated with Text: https://www.youtube.com/watch?v=CblhxhnSymg

556. Book Text: *LibreOffice-Writer (1) A First Look* Link Associated with Text: https://www.youtube.com/watch?v=mc845_FuONY

557. Book Text: *How to Write a Perfect Memo* Link Associated with Text: https://www.youtube.com/watch?v=G_jErsVxjpM

558. Book Text: *Purdue Online Writing Lab (OWL* Link Associated with Text: https://owl.purdue.edu/owl/purdue_owl.html

559. Book Text: *Video: Purdue OWL: Visual Rhetoric* Link Associated with Text: https://www.youtube.com/watch?v=-vJvivIzkDg

560. Book Text: *How Isaac Newton helped shape our coins* Link Associated with Text: http://blog.perthmint.com.au/2015/09/29/how-isaac-newton-helped-shape-our-coins/

561. Book Text: *Top 10 Isaac Newton Inventions: The Perfect Coin* Link Associated with Text: https://science.howstuffworks.com/innovation/famous-inventors/5-isaac-newton-inventions8.htm

562. Book Text: *Methods of coin debasement, Wikipedia* Link Associated with Text: https://en.wikipedia.org/wiki/Methods_of_coin_debasement

563. Book Text: *The Royal Mint Museum, Issac Newton* Link Associated with Text: http://www.royalmintmuseum.org.uk/history/people/mint-officials/isaac-newton/index.html

564. Book Text: *Frick Collection* Link Associated with Text: https://www.frick.org/

565. Book Text: *Andrew Carnegie* Link Associated with Text: https://en.wikipedia.org/wiki/Andrew_Carnegie

566. Book Text: *Frick is reported to have responded* Link Associated with Text: https://www.npr.org/templates/story/story.php?storyId=4717704

567. Book Text: *Henry Clay Frick* Link Associated with Text: https://www.frick.org/about/history/henry_clay_frick

568. Book Text: *Henry Clay Frick, Wikipedia* Link Associated with Text: https://en.wikipedia.org/wiki/Henry_Clay_Frick

569. Book Text: *Henry Clay Frick (1849-1919)* Link Associated with Text: https://www.pbs.org/wgbh/americanexperience/features/goldman-henry-clay-frick-1849-1919/

570.   Book Text: *Frick, Henry Clay* Link Associated with Text:
http://www.anb.org/view/10.1093/anb/9780198606697.001.0001/anb-9780198606697-e-1000597

571.   Book Text: *Video: Introduction to The Frick Collection* Link
Associated with Text:
https://www.youtube.com/watch?v=LEyC8g94MZE

572.   Book Text: *National Parks of the United States* Link Associated with
Text: https://www.nps.gov/findapark/index.htm

573.   Book Text: *Glacier National Park* Link Associated with Text:
https://www.nps.gov/glac/index.htm

574.   Book Text: *Video: Scenic Hikes in Eastern Glacier National Park*
Link Associated with Text:
https://www.youtube.com/watch?v=BxikeSMhXXY

www.ingramcontent.com/pod-product-compliance
Lightning Source LLC
Chambersburg PA
CBHW041221270326
41932CB00006B/45